modern retro
tabletop

modern retro
tabletop

living with mid-century tableware

RYLAND
PETERS
& SMALL
LONDON NEW YORK

madeleine marsh

with photography by **thomas stewart**

Designer Luis Peral-Aranda
Senior editor Sophie Bevan
Location research manager Kate Brunt
Production Patricia Harrington
Art director Gabriella Le Grazie
Publishing director Alison Starling

Stylist Siri Hills
Period props researched and sourced by Luis Peral-Aranda

First published in the United Kingdom in 2002
by Ryland Peters & Small
Kirkman House
12–14 Whitfield Street
London W1T 2RP
www.rylandpeters.com

10 9 8 7 6 5 4 3 2 1

ISBN 1 84172 127 1

A CIP record for this book is available from the British Library.

CONTENTS

INTRODUCTION

The aim of
this book is to explore the changing
tastes in tableware from the 1940s to the 1970s,
and to show how these vintage objects can be stylishly
incorporated into the modern interior. One of the joys of collecting
retro tableware, is the pleasure of living with it. This is not a book about
precious antiques, frozen in time and locked away in a display cabinet. Whilst
some of the period pieces shown are purely decorative, many more are still
performing the ordinary domestic tasks for which they were created, perhaps half a
century ago. Standing alongside contemporary products on kitchen worktops, dining-room
tables and living-room sideboards, these are collectables that are used and actively
enjoyed. Though they might have been designed in the past, they work in the present – living
proof that good design is timeless. The book is divided into two parts. The first sets tableware
in its period context. It looks at the major media – ceramics, glass, metalware, wood, plastic –
and explores postwar developments in pattern, shape and colour. But this is not just a
history of the applied arts. With the end of World War II, came a huge period of change.
The objects displayed chart the move from '40s austerity to '50s affluence. They reflect
the ephemeral Pop styles of the urban, swinging '60s and the brown and oatmeal
countrified look of the back-to-nature '70s. By its very nature, tableware tells
the story of the people who used it: what they ate and drank, how they
decorated their homes, how they entertained, their fashions,
aspirations and lifestyles. These everyday items – mugs,
plates, knives and forks – provide not just a
decorative picture of their

times, but

also a social history and a hands-on,

three-dimensional link with the past. The second part

of this book goes into present-day houses and apartments

where retro tableware is used and displayed. Every home tells its own

decorative story. We look at the effect that new and exotic foodstuffs had on

the domestic tabletop. We meet the Scandinavian designers who exported teak

furnishings and rational Modernism to homes across the world. We witness the birth of

the modern kitchen with its shiny chrome, American-style appliances. And we chart the

extravagance of '60s fashions, from Italian space-age plastics to British Pop-art products.

Contrasting with these glowing psychedelic interiors, is the more natural and neutral look of a

country-style kitchen, with its bare wood and '70s handcrafted pottery: a modern return to our

rural past. In these living rooms, kitchens and dining rooms, tableware is included from across the

world, reflecting the global nature of postwar shopping. Furnishing and decoration encompasses

a variety of tastes and reflects both the past and the present. However, these are not museum

settings or time capsules, but real homes where vintage and contemporary pieces are combined.

Purist collectors might insist on an original American food-mixer or a period Arne Jacobsen

kitchen chair, but equally some of these objects have never gone out of production. In

some instances (such as electrical kitchen appliances), whilst you might want a

period look, you might not want old equipment, and a modern version of

a vintage design can provide the perfect and practical solution. The

accent here is not to recreate the past, but to live with it in

the present, drawing on a range of periods, places,

objects and influences to create a uniquely

personal style.

ELEMENTS OF THE RETRO TABLETOP

01 MATERIALS | 02 COLOURS | 03 SHAPES | 04 PATTERNS

CERAMICS

Once wartime restrictions were lifted, the demand for ceramics boomed. In America, industrial ceramic designers such as Eva Zeisel and Russel Wright were pioneering new shapes and colours in everyday crockery. Inspired by their work, Finnish designer Kaj Franck and the Midwinter factory in Britain also created some of the most innovative tableware of the '50s, designed to meet the needs of a new generation of homeowners.

Iroquois Casual China designed by Russel Wright in 1946 came in mix-and-match colours, many named after food (sugar white, lettuce green, ripe apricot). Some shades, such as lemon yellow and parsley green, were withdrawn earlier than others, making them harder to find today.

ABOVE Reflecting the rise in popularity of instant coffee and the tea bag, the mug took over from the cup and saucer. These were made by the British firm Hornsea (established in 1949), who achieved huge success in the '60s and '70s with their mass-produced pottery that nevertheless retained a handmade, country feel.

ABOVE RIGHT Kaj Franck's Kilta range was produced in 1953 for Arabia in five mix-and-match glazes – white, black, green, blue and yellow. The waisted glass carafe was also designed by Franck circa 1955, and came in different colours.

BELOW These large pottery vases were made in 1955 by the French ceramicist Georges Jouve.

Russel Wright's American Modern dinnerware, which retailed over 80 million pieces, introduced rimless plates and curvaceous streamlined pots to countless American homes in the '40s and '50s. In 1946, he created another bestseller with his Iroquois Casual China, featuring oven-to-table ware perfect for the kitchen-diner. Like American Modern, Iroquois was produced in different colours that the housewife could mix and match as she expanded her china along with her family. Wright's mix-and-match tableware was a major influence on Kaj Franck. His Kilta range designed for Arabia in 1953 came in clear coordinating colours and simple standardized shapes. Stackable, affordable and multifunctional, Kilta was the answer for those living in flats or smaller homes and embracing an informal – and servantless – lifestyle.

Alongside this focus on mass production, there was a growing interest in individual craftsmanship. Major commercial factories, such as Gustavsberg in Sweden and Poole in England, also ran artistic studios where designers experimented with extravagant organic shapes, hand-painted colours and new textures. In the '60s, small, independent potteries flourished, and fashionable urban shops, from Williams-Sonoma in San Francisco to Habitat in London, sold traditional French country earthenware.

Ceramic tableware reflected the postwar revolution in food and drink: the introduction of new products, foreign foods and more relaxed eating habits. Perhaps the ultimate symbol of this new informality was the mug. Decorated with anything from abstract patterns to political slogans, mugs could be mixed, without having to match at all.

THIS PAGE The organic influence pervaded not just the shape of mid-century modern ceramics but also their texture. These Reptile relief-moulded bowls and vase, inspired by lizard skin, were produced in the '50s by Stig Lindberg for the Swedish firm Gustavsberg. Inventive and varied, Lindberg's works are very sought after today.

Glassware from different periods can be mixed and matched without losing a cohesive retro feel. Here amber glass – a '70s favourite – appears in many forms, including a clear Holmegaard bottle vase – or 'Gulvase', as they were called – and modern stemware designed by Bowles and Linares which comes in two parts – a round-based vessel nestling in an elegant stand. Their elongated shapes fit perfectly with the tall vintage pieces.

MATERIALS

GLASS

Italy and Northern Europe dominated decorative glass design in the '50s and '60s. For centuries, the island of Murano in Venice had been a major centre of glassmaking. Reviving ancient ornamental techniques, Venetian glassmaker Paolo Venini produced his famous series of handkerchief vases, folding squares of free-blown glass like napkins, and creating one of the most distinctive and most imitated shapes of the '50s.

Italian glass was noted for its brilliant colour and bold fanciful shapes at every level of the market, from the finest art glass to low-cost decorative ware. Minor workshops catered to the tourist trade, turning out multicoloured glass fish and multi-layered sommerso ashtrays, a favourite on the '60s coffee table.

Scandinavian glassmakers adopted a cooler, more rational approach, creating both studio glass and mass-produced utilitarian ware with equal commitment. Working for Iittala, Finnish designer Timo Sarpaneva won awards both for his glass sculptures and his functional i-line tableware, for which he designed everything from drinking vessels to packaging. Moving on from the smooth free-blown shapes of the '50s, Sarpaneva and his fellow designer Tapio Wirkkala experimented with texture. Glass was blown in wooden moulds, creating a bark-like surface that became a distinctive feature of '60s table glass. In addition to Iittala and Nuutajärvi in Finland, leading Nordic factories included Kosta and Orrefors in Sweden and Holmegaard in Denmark, where artistic director Per Lütken created handsome organic designs.

While art glass flourished, developments in the manufacture of heat-resistant glass also affected everyday kitchenware. The Schott factory in West Germany produced glass casseroles and drinking vessels using a new, fully automatic process. Corning in the USA introduced coloured and decorated Pyrex dishes to attract the housewife, and one of the most coveted appliances in the '50s kitchen was an American-style electric oven, complete with a glass panel (a hugely popular innovation) through which you could keep an eye on your cooking.

'Handicrafts and industrial production go hand in hand. We need human design, sensitivity and the power of machines.' Timo Sarpaneva

FAR LEFT The tea set with a removable infuser was originally conceived in 1931 by Bauhaus designer Wilhelm Wagenfeld for the Schott factory in Jena, Germany, who were pioneers in the development of heat-resistant glass. After World War II, and funded by the Marshall plan, the factory was moved to Mainz in West Germany and fully automated. Wagenfeld's design was reworked by Heinrich Löffelhardt to suit machine-operated presses, which permitted the use of much thinner glass, as seen in this postwar service.

LEFT This Italian vase dates from the '50s. Attributed to Venini, it reflects the Italian taste for glowing colours and extravagant glass techniques.

ABOVE These red-and-white cased-glass Gulvases were designed by Otto Brauer for Holmegaard Glassworks in Denmark in the '60s. They were also manufactured in clear glass *(page 17)*, though cased examples with a white lining tend to command higher prices in today's market place.

MATERIALS
METALWARE

Metal was a favourite postwar medium. In the '50s, designers exploited its linear and organic qualities; in the '60s, it took on a shiny space-age feel, appearing in every form, from tubular coffee pots to chain-mail mini skirts. At the Festival of Britain in 1951, the Skylon, an aluminium-and-steel sculpture, towering 90 metres above the South Bank in London, heralded a new look in metalware: a spindly graphic line, expressed in the wire fruit baskets, plant holders and magazine racks that filled '50s living rooms.

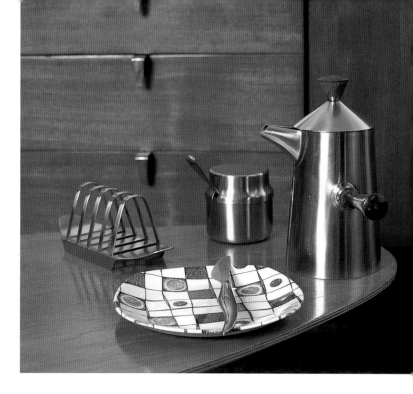

Stainless steel, initially developed for the armaments industry, was transformed from an industrial material into elegant tableware to rival silver.

American-style chrome appliances became popular in the kitchen, and stainless steel replaced silverware on the most glamorous tabletops. British designer Robert Welch drew on his experience as a silversmith to create a whole range of stainless-steel services in contemporary designs for Old Hall Tableware, produced by J & J Wiggin Ltd, the first British firm to manufacture stainless-steel tableware. Welch won

Design Centre awards for his Campden tableware in 1958 and his Alveston range in 1965. Campden (circa 1956) was a joint design with David Mellor, who produced some of the most influential cutlery of the postwar period, ranging from the slender Pride in 1953 (which combined a contemporary look with a traditional Georgian feel) to Thrift in 1965 (an economical setting designed for HM prisons and hospitals) and Chinese Black in 1975 (made from strip steel with resin handles, its chunky graphic look became an icon of '70s style).

Still in Europe, inventive modern silver was produced by Italian designer Lino Sabattini and Danish sculptor Henning Koppel, whose curvilinear pitchers for Georg Jensen made metal look like a living substance. 'When I see how a branch grows organically out of the trunk of a tree, I am inspired by this,' explained Koppel. 'I seek to create the same organic unity between the body of a jug and its spout.' The firms of Gense in Sweden and Stelton in Denmark exported Scandinavian stainless steel across the world. Among Stelton's most famous products was the Cylinda Line tableware *(pages 67 and 99)* designed by Arne Jacobsen – a service of gleaming, geometrical cylinders that captured the shiny spirit of the '60s.

In 1954, Danish designer Jens Quistgaard and American entrepreneur Ted Nierenberg founded Dansk Designs to market Scandinavian style in the USA. 'From peasant craft to a sophisticated line … Dansk wooden pieces are up to the minute in design, practical and exquisitely crafted,' noted one contemporary critic. Scandinavia also promoted the '60s fashion for wooden-handled cutlery, only ousted from the dining room by the arrival of the dishwasher in the kitchen.

While Scandinavian designers sought to give a modern twist to a traditional material, in the later '60s and '70s there was a craving for a more rustic look. '50s Formica was ripped out in favour of wooden panels and stripped-pine tables, as even urban homeowners opted for farmhouse style. 'The kitchen should be the most comforting and comfortable room in the house,' advised cookery writer Elizabeth David, whose London kitchenware shop, opened in 1965, sold the same French wooden bowls, mandolins and chopping boards that formed part of her own influential *batterie de cuisine*. Terence Conran's *The Kitchen Book* (1977) recommended the purchase of beech salad servers and elm salad bowls. 'Imagine a fresh green salad in an orange plastic bowl,' he noted with distaste. The interest in country tableware grew, and wooden items imported from peasant cultures across the globe decorated the most stylish metropolitan tables.

OPPOSITE **Against a wooden sculpture by Brian Willsher is a wooden-cased clock by George Nelson, one of America's most influential postwar designers. From 1949, Nelson produced a range of designs for the Howard Miller Clock Company.**
LEFT **This cheeseboard and ice bucket are by Skjøde Knudsen for Skjøde Skjern circa 1960.**
BELOW LEFT **This ice bucket is by Finn Juhl circa 1958. The salad servers and tray are by Jens Quistgaard for Dansk. Combining industrial techniques with hand-craftsmanship, Quistgaard's wooden tableware was solid, stylish, contemporary, and today is highly collectable.**

If one material typified the Scandinavian Modern look in the '50s and early '60s, it was wood, particularly teak. Denmark, in particular, used this wood to produce high-quality, sophisticated furniture and domestic items, which were exported across the world.

MATERIALS
WOOD

Plastic technology, developed during World War II, revolutionized peace-time products and the look of the contemporary home. Not only was it break-resistant, but it could also be moulded into user-friendly shapes.

PLASTICS

In the '50s kitchen, Formica worktops and vinyl coverings attracted housewives with the promise of bright modern colours and easy-clean surfaces. 'Want a miracle floor – a sparkling plastic wonder that glows with beauty and laughs at dirt?' seduced a typical advertisement. Overcoming early difficulties with melting and fading, manufacturers recommended plastic tableware as the perfect product for the rough and tumble of family life.

Melamine, refined in the '40s when the US Navy commissioned unbreakable dishes for maritime use, was a favourite '50s choice. Russel Wright's Residential melamine dinnerware, launched in 1953, combined fluid organic shapes with a range of fashionable colours, and came with a 10-year guarantee against breakage. A host of manufacturers entered the melamine market, and by 1960, *Good Housekeeping* magazine claimed that one in four American families owned a set of plastic dishes.

In the '60s, plastic moved from the kitchen to the living room, with plastic furniture. Italy, Germany and Scandinavia were all leading producers of stylish pieces. While manufacturers were keen to stress its elegance, plastic was also the perfect medium for cheap and cheerful products, including many icons of period kitsch. Even at its most practical, an element of fun was often introduced: the success of Tupperware, created by American scientist Earl S. Tupper in 1945, was due as much to the invention of the Tupperware party as it was to the patented airtight seal.

OPPOSITE This plastic
Thermos, creamer and
sugar bowl are by Danish
designer Erik Magnussen,
who worked for Stelton
in the '70s.

ABOVE This parmesan
dish was designed in
1968 by Enzo Mari for the
Italian company Danese.
This is a modern reissue,
produced for Alessi.

RIGHT This Helit German
ashtray typifies the bold
shapes and bright colours
of '60s and '70s plastics.

ABOVE One of the reasons for the success of
melamine was that it could take strong dyes, as
exhibited by this orange-and-white Gaydon service.

THIS PAGE **The Nature Study service was created by Terence Conran for Midwinter in 1955. The matte-black glaze showed off the curvaceous lines of Midwinter's new Fashion shape and contrasted with white saucers decorated with sketches of leaves and butterflies.**

OPPOSITE ABOVE **Eva Zeisel's expressively organic Town and Country cruets were produced for Red Wing Pottery USA in 1946.**

OPPOSITE BELOW **These black-and-white plates were all designed by Jessie Tait for Midwinter circa 1955–56. The patterns are Monaco (top), Tonga (right), and Zambesi (left). Zambesi was a very popular design and inspired many imitations.**

The crisp definition of black and white was a favourite choice for a young generation setting up home. 'Cream was what your parents had,' remembers one '50s homeowner. 'Black and white was clean, sharp and modern. It was the New Look.'

BLACK AND WHITE

Monochrome designs appeared on everything, from textiles to tableware, and in every style, from figurative to abstract. White saucers decorated with free-handed sketches were coordinated with black cups and coffee pots, the all-over colour emphasizing the silhouette of the new, organic shapes.

Contemporary designers brought art to the tabletop. Piero Fornasetti's *trompe l'œil* black-and-white plates *(pages 10–11)*, were inspired by both surrealism and historical prints. In contrast, American ceramicist Eva Zeisel drew on the biomorphic forms of contemporary abstract sculptures to produce her Town and Country tableware. Black-and-white textiles, spattered with dots and dashes, mirrored the 'drip and splash' canvases of Jackson Pollock.

A spindly black graphic line was a characteristic feature of '50s style, expressing itself three-dimensionally in wirework furniture and decorative objects, as well as on flat surfaces. Ceramics were covered with scratchy, hand-painted black lines, and the '50s saw a craze for zebra-striped tableware, paving the way for the Op-art fashions that were to follow in the '60s. Pioneered by painters including Bridget Riley and Victor Vasarely, Optical Art used geometrical abstraction to disrupt and fragment the vision, creating the illusion of movement. The necessary mechanical precision made it a style ripe for mass production, and, sometimes to the dismay of its fine-art originators, dizzying black-and-white 'Op' patterns decorated domestic items from tablecloths to drinking glasses.

Polystyrene canisters and melamine tableware came in every conceivable shade, and manufacturers boasted that husbands could choose a Formica tabletop to match their wife's eyes! Even the most functional appliances no longer had to be white. American fridges came with coloured doors; everything from food-mixers to ice crushers were made in a range of 'gay' colours.

'Mix and match' was a favourite term, with tableware produced in coordinating combinations. Two-tone ceramics became fashionable (one colour inside, another outside), as did 'harlequin' tea and coffee sets, in which every guest could have a different cup and saucer. 'Never before has the hostess had so many colours to choose from,' thrilled one '50s woman's journal, and magazines offered helpful advice on how to mix tableware 'like paints on a palette', even suggesting dressing to match the dishes.

Once rationing finally came to an end, food and drink, too, became more decorative. The return of the cocktail party brought colourful drinks served in equally bright 'domino' cocktail glasses, the theory being that if everybody had a different glass, no matter how much you drank, you would remember which one was yours! 'A buffet table should display a colourful array of refreshments … exciting enough to make "conversation pieces",' advised a typical period cookbook, in which every dish was smothered with a multicoloured garnish. But if culinary fashions could veer to extremes, tastes in tableware were more sophisticated. Objects came in complementary tones – pastel shades were a '50s favourite – mixed but still matching, and paving the way for the clashing colours of the psychedelic '60s.

COLOURS
MULTICOLOURED

LEFT These tea cups in blue, green, pink and yellow reflect the '50s fashion for mix-and-match tableware.

BELOW Hornsea slipware vases in mauve, green and yellow demonstrate the trend for delicate, pastel colours in the home.

RIGHT Two-tone tableware (one colour within, another without) was a period favourite, both in ceramics and other media. These bowls, made from steel with bright enamel interiors, are Danish Krenit ware. They were designed in 1953 by Herbert Krenchel and manufactured by Torben Ørskov.

After the drabness of war, there was a huge lust for colour in the home. Plastics, in particular, helped transform the kitchen from a sterile white zone into – according to the advertisements – a colourful, wipe-clean playground.

NATURALS AND NEUTRALS

The rampant artifice of many '50s products, with their use of plastics, metal and acid colours, was countered by a more naturalistic approach. Scandinavia, in particular, while pioneering some of the most experimental design of the period, also remained firmly committed to a culture of traditional craftsmanship and native materials. Landscape was a major source of inspiration, offering strong textures and colours that were earthy and neutral.

'We feel that nature is the true source of lasting beauty,' explained Finnish designer Kaj Franck, 'does anyone ever tire of looking at a graceful birch … or a beautiful sunset?' Glass reflecting snow and ice, wooden tableware, hand-thrown pots and hand-woven, natural textiles all became part of the Scandinavian Modern look, adopted around the world.

As changing eating habits were reflected in tableware, the '60s interest in health food and vegetarianism was matched by a desire for equally natural and healthy-looking receptacles.

The Craftsmen Potters Association, London's most fashionable shop for handmade ceramics, was opened in the same street and by the same person as the capital's most trendy vegetarian café, 'Cranks' – its name deliberately parodying the health-food fad. Small potteries, such as Rye and Troika, flourished, and even the big commercial companies sought to give mass-produced crockery a handmade, earthenware feel. If the '60s palette was psychedelic, it was also brown, cream and oatmeal, the colours of muesli.

MAIN IMAGE **The Home Décor range of vases was designed by John Clappison for Hornsea Pottery in 1960.**
INSET **The Poole Twintone coffee service dates from the '50s. The mottled grey 'seagull' glaze was matched with a range of plain colours, here brown. Neutral in colour and contemporary in shape, Twintone was a very successful line.**

TECHNICOLOUR

If '50s colours were harmoniously mixed and matched, in the '60s every colour of the rainbow could be blended together.

THIS PAGE **Even the most functional kitchenware was sprinkled with psychedelic flowers. The shaker and rolling pin are from the Gaytime range by Lord Nelson Pottery, UK; the casserole is by Figgjo Tableware in Norway; and the floral canisters are from Staffordshire Potteries.**

Influenced by Pop art, designers favoured bright tones and a hard-edged graphic style. Classic motifs include the target, the Union Jack and blow-up numbers and letters – images stripped of their traditional significance and applied to domestic items in glorious technicolour. Red, white and blue was a favourite '60s combination and a symbol of Carnaby Style. If 'Swinging London' was the centre of Pop and Mod fashion, then 'Dreaming California' (notably, San Francisco), was the birthplace of psychedelia, inspired by hallucinogenic drugs, spread by the hippy movement, and expressing itself in every form, from music to posters to tableware. Whitefriars glass Bark vases *(page 89),* launched in 1967, the year of the summer of love, came in a range of technicolour hues, including Kingfisher Blue, Tangerine and Lilac. Orange, purple and pink were popular decorative shades, appearing on the most mundane objects, from storage tins to rolling pins. In Britain, Morphy Richards manufactured an orange toaster decorated with shocking-pink Mary Quant daisies. Marimekko, Finland's leading textile firm, produced glowing furnishing and dress fabrics in Op-art patterns, offering total immersion in multicoloured spots and stripes.

OPPOSITE **The target was a major Pop-art emblem. American artist Jasper Johns became famous for his target paintings in the '50s, and by the following decade, the target motif was seen on everything from tee shirts to record covers. This plate was designed and produced by British designer Paul Clark in 1965, and shows how Pop symbols even filtered through to '60s tableware.**

RIGHT Curving vessels by Poole Pottery UK, who experimented with contemporary freeform designs in the '50s.

FAR RIGHT ABOVE This white bowl with a turquoise interior is by Mitzi Cunliffe, who created a series of sculptural, asymmetric shapes for Pilkington Pottery in the UK in the early '50s.

FAR RIGHT BELOW Dishes from the Century range designed in 1957 for Hall China USA by Eva Zeisel, a pioneer of organic modernism in tableware.

SHAPES
ORGANIC

After the severity of '30s modernism and wartime austerity, there was a desire for soft and swelling feminine forms. The kidney-shaped coffee table was a '50s favourite, and similar rounded designs appeared in every medium. The popularity of this amoeba-like form has been attributed to new scientific discoveries (microscopic views of molecules), to camouflage patterns, and to the influence of modern painting.

Tableware was stripped of dirt-catching angles and decorations. Innovations included the rimless plate, its soft-cornered shape poised between square and circle, providing a perfect surface for all-over decoration and bringing an end to the English habit of putting salt on the edge. Jugs and teapots swelled like pregnant women. Curves replaced straight lines and asymmetry was a distinctive feature. The Poole coffee set *(page 33)* literally reflects the waisted, hourglass shape, its base flowing out like a circle skirt.

Centres of organic design included Scandinavia, where nature was a major creative influence, and America, home of new technology and manmade materials. Though inspired by nature, organic shapes did not necessitate organic materials – plastic was perfect for biomorphic forms.

THIS PAGE **A keynote of organic design, with its undulating, freeform shapes, is a balance between art and nature. These white vases, by Swedish designers Stig Lindberg and Gunnar Nylund, suggest both abstract sculpture and the shapes of shells or seed pods. Working for Gustavsberg, Lindberg was inspired by nature both in terms of form and decoration, and in the '50s created a range of painted vessels based on leaf designs.**

Fashion and furnishing often go hand in hand. If the classic '50s silhouette was the hourglass, epitomized by Christian Dior's 'New Look', then design in the home was equally curvilinear.

SHAPES
GEOMETRIC

If the '50s were curvaceous, then the '60s were streamlined. This look was perhaps most famously embodied by Twiggy, leading model of the day and teenage icon of swinging London, with her waif-like boyish figure, short haircut and long, mini-skirted legs.

As in fashion, tastes in tableware veered to the tall, slim and tubular. The can-shaped coffee pot, pioneered by British designer Susie Cooper in the '50s, became a favourite feature on the '60s table. The simple cylinder provided a perfect medium for all manner of decorations. Portmeirion, who adopted the can shape in 1962, decorated services with everything from the Greek Key motif to Victorian prints *(page 104)*. Their slender coffee pots towered some 35 centimetres high. 'I had to stand up to pour out the coffee,' remembers one '60s housewife.

Everywhere, '50s organic flowing forms were replaced by straight-sided vessels and simple geometric shapes – oval and quartic plates gave way to circles, and the cone was a popular shape for cruet sets. Flush lids also enhanced the clean geometric lines; this feature contributed to the look of Arne Jacobsen's Cylinda Line stainless-steel tableware *(pages 67 and 89)*, which – from pots to packaging – was entirely based round the cylinder. Designers experimented with the geometric look throughout different media. In cutlery, there was a fashion for thick, short-pronged forks, asymmetric knives, large, shallow-bowled spoons and salad servers terminating in flat discs. Carafes with elongated necks and geometric-shaped vases were a feature of contemporary glassware, their abstracted forms complemented by jubilantly psychedelic colours.

OPPOSITE **This Hornsea service is typical of its time both in its shape and the use of flat lids. Removing the knop not only simplified the silhouette of jugs and canisters, but also made them cheaper to produce, easier to stack and harder to damage.**
ABOVE **These German porcelain demi-tasses show that cups, too, followed the tall, cylindrical look.**
ABOVE LEFT **This ceramic bottle vase is by Guido Gambone, one of Italy's leading postwar potters.**

THIS PAGE **A porcelain service created by German designer Nick Roericht in 1959 and manufactured in the US by Thomas China and Crystal from 1961. Space-saving tableware was much in demand, and this stackable dinnerware, designed when Roericht was still a student, was widely admired and much imitated.**

'Espresso coffee was to the '50s what marijuana was to the '60s, the drug of choice for a generation,' remembered Terence Conran. The '50s saw the rise of the Italian coffee bar, favourite teenage hangout, with its bright Formica tables, juke box and gleaming chrome espresso machine. Taste for coffee filtered through to the home, resulting in a huge variety of grinders, pots and percolators.

Thanks to increased prosperity, and the introduction of hire-purchase schemes, sales of electrical equipment boomed. Kitchens were increasingly filled with labour-saving appliances: fridges, food mixers, toasters. American machines, with their glamorous curves and bold automotive styling, gave way by the end of the '50s to more minimal, rational shapes inspired by German design. Space was at a premium in the smaller homes and flats built in the postwar period, hence the development of stackable dinner sets, fitted kitchens and sleeker domestic appliances. Bernadotte & Bjørn's 1950 nesting 'Margrethe' bowls were among the earliest melamine items produced in Scandinavia, and are still in production today. Easy to store, hard to break and light to lift, these stylish, heat-resistant bowls came in different colours and were a perfect addition to the contemporary kitchen.

New technology in the living room also affected eating habits. With the introduction of the television, families abandoned the dining table in favour of snacking in front of the box. Ceramic manufacturers responded by introducing a combined cup and plate, marketed as a 'telly set'. Television not only created demand for instant food; it advertised it, too. In America, Swanson's came up with the first TV dinner in 1953. Vesta curries and paellas – 'just add water' – first appeared on British supermarket shelves in 1961, and, 'ready in only 20 minutes', introduced many to their first taste of foreign food.

Cheaper travel and the growth of the package holiday in the '60s stimulated interest in the cuisine of other countries, as did the surge in foreign restaurants. Avocado dishes and fondue sets became new additions to the middle-class wedding list. Fashionable '60s kitchen equipment included French Le Creuset casseroles, Greek olive-wood salad bowls and tall glass jars for Italian spaghetti, reflecting the diversity and increasingly global nature of home cooking.

New forms in tableware reflected fashions in food as increased prosperity brought greater choice to the table.

SHAPES

NEW FORMS FOR NEW FUNCTIONS

TOP **Bernadotte and Bjørn's nesting Margrethe bowls proved that plastic could be a serious rival to more traditional materials. The designers examined many vessels before coming up with their final ergonomic form, which included an integral handle and spout and a rubber ring to stop the bowl from slipping.**
ABOVE **In the '20s and '30s, combined cups and plates were known as 'breakfast' or 'tennis' sets. In the '50s, they were relaunched as 'telly sets'; this example is by Denby Potteries.**

This '50s tray (resting on a Conran table) is a laminated textile design by Lucienne Day. The linear abstract pattern and acid colours are typical of the era.

ABSTRACT

Abstract patterns flourished on postwar tableware, reflecting contemporary art, modern scientific imagery and the new shapes of the space age.

Abstraction entered the home through domestic designers. 'People who would never have hung an abstract painting on their walls, hung the boldest abstract curtains on their windows. It was a very exciting time,' remembers British designer Lucienne Day, who created some of the most important textiles of the '50s. Day's influences included painters such as Joan Miró and Paul Klee, and contemporary art affected every medium. Scandinavian glass echoed the sculptural forms produced by Constantin Brancusi and Henry Moore. Ceramic tableware was decorated with geometric shapes and abstract expressionist doodles.

'50s abstract patterns are often characterized by fluid, organic forms and a sinuous, hand-drawn line. In the '60s, this linear delicacy gave way to bigger, bolder shapes and a more rigid geometry. Barbara Brown's Focus pattern *(see page 108)* is a carefully controlled design of squares and circles, favourite

These dinner plates are all by Midwinter. The Chequers pattern (below) was produced by Terence Conran first as a textile, then in 1957 as a tableware design. The free-hand pattern with its uneven lines and sketchy motifs reflects the humane approach to abstraction characteristic of '50s style. A similarly random effect also appears in the designs created by Jessie Tait (opposite): **Mosaic** (top right) **and Homespun** (bottom), created in the early '60s, and **Magic Moments** (top left) from the '50s. INSET '60s abstraction in art translated well to tableware, as proved in this Op-art dish.

motifs of the period. Abstraction became increasingly slick and mechanical through the '60s, with Pop-art motifs and Op-art patterns.

If modern art was one major influence on abstract design, another was contemporary science. From the discovery of DNA to the detonation of the H-bomb, this was the 'atomic age'. The world of hidden shapes revealed in the microscope was a huge source of inspiration. The Festival Pattern Group's imagery, based on crystal structures, for the Festival of Britain (1951) stimulated a fashion for molecular designs.

Science affected shape as well as pattern. George Nelson's 1949 Ball wall clock, a starburst form of metal rods and wooden spheres, was based on 3D models of atomic structure. This 'line and blob' look (also known as the cocktail-cherry style) filtered throughout '50s design, from black wirework fruit baskets standing on colourful ball feet to the mighty Atomium, central building of the 1958 Brussels Expo, a model of an iron molecule 110 metres high. Space exploration took designers higher still, with shiny plastic, stainless steel and strong geometric shapes filling the home.

FIGURATIVE AND FLORAL

The '50s fashion for decoration resulted in a wealth of figurative designs celebrating modern life. Ceramics illustrated with pictures of fresh food marked the end of wartime shortages. Contemporary furnishing was another favourite subject: images of leggy plant stands and boomerang tables appeared on dinner plates. And with the return of European travel, manufacturers reflected the desire for Continental glamour with Riviera scenes and pictures of chic Parisian ladies.

The British manufacturer Midwinter sent artist Hugh Casson to the south of France in 1953/4; his festive watercolours of ports and cafés resulted in the bestselling Cannes (shown here) **and Riviera ceramics.**

A new age needed a new decorative vocabulary. The animals that expressed the '50s were the French poodle and the long-necked cat, appearing in every form, from tea cups to tablecloths. Rejecting traditional florals, designers examined flowers with the analytical eye of a scientist. Terence Conran drew on his juvenile experience as a lepidopterist to produce the ceramic pattern Nature Study *(page 28)* in 1954, reducing plants and insects to black-and-white skeletal structures. In Jessie Tait's Flower Mist, the naïve,

almost abstracted, blooms are again pared down to the minimum.

The '60s saw a more 'Pop' approach to nature. Perhaps the most famous flower of the decade was Mary Quant's daisy, which not only appeared on all her fashion products, but sprung up throughout the decorative arts. As the hippy revolution shook the world, flower power blossomed, and the slick, graphic daisy gave way to swirling tendrils and fantastical blooms.

The '50s and '60s saw the rise of the teenager, and as young people gained more spending power, so manufacturers catered to their interests. Tableware was decorated with rock-and-roll images and Beatles fans could drink from Fab Four glasses and eat from Beatles plates. In an age of protest and slogans, typography also became an important decorative form. Mugs were featured blow-up numbers and letters, and fashionable companies, such as tinware manufacture Dodo Designs and Portmeirion Pottery, revived Victorian imagery with a Carnaby Street twist *(pages 104–7)*.

OPPOSITE '50s Midwinter plates demonstrate the fashion in floral and botanical decoration. Terence Conran's 1955 Salad Ware (below left) shows colourful sketches of vegetables, providing a celebratory record of changing eating habits. Plant Life (top left), again by Conran, circa 1956, reflects the period craze for indoor pot plants. While pre-war ceramics are often decorated with springtime forms and colours, '50s tastes were more autumnal. Falling Leaves (top right) was designed by Jessie Tait in 1955 and Flower Mist (bottom right) was produced by Tait in 1956.
LEFT Susie Cooper, who had remained in the vanguard of ceramic trends since the '20s, produced the Carnaby Daisy coffee set in 1968, clearly inspired by Mary Quant's logo and the swinging London scene.
ABOVE Springtime china was manufactured by Hornsea in the '60s and provides a variation on the favourite daisy motif.

LIVING WITH RETRO TABLEWARE

THE POSTWAR LOOK

With the end of World War II came a pressing need for new housing and an equally powerful desire for a new style of furnishing. Technologies developed during the war revolutionized the peacetime interior. Steel, plywood and plastic were used to meet the demand for more flexible, space-saving and affordable domestic objects. A young generation of architects and designers, inspired by abstract art and scientific progress, transformed the postwar home with New Look design.

LEFT **Some of the best in European and American design can be seen here. The shelving system by French designers Jean Prouvé and Charlotte Perriand dates from 1953 and offers the perfect means to display eclectic pieces of the time. On the top shelf are vases by Jean Cocteau, and the white '50s wavy-rimmed planter on the shelf beneath is by Poole. The freeform bowl below that is by American-born sculptor Mitzi Cunliffe, who designed a range of thick-walled, asymmetric and sculptural ceramics for Pilkington Tile and Pottery Company in the early '50s.**
RIGHT **Slatted benches, which could serve either as tables or seating, were a popular feature of the period. This Tokyo bench, designed by Charlotte Perriand, displays large pottery vases in bright contrasting tones created by French ceramicist Georges Jouve.**

Clear and colourful, this interior conjures up the new 'contemporary' look of the early '50s with its combination of bold organic shapes and fine graphic lines. The postwar fashion for open-plan rooms and more flexible living arrangements was reflected in modern furnishing – lightness and mobility were a key feature.

In 1944, American architect George Nelson (pioneer of the indoor shopping mall) came up with the concept of 'storagewall', a series of multi-purpose, mix-and-match storage units that sounded the deathknell for the traditional sideboard. Combining display shelves and cupboards (often multicoloured like an abstract painting), these versatile systems were produced by everyone from leading international designers to mass-manufacturers. The structure could either be placed free-standing, serving as a room divider between living and dining areas, or stood against the wall, as shown here. The lines of the unit contrast with the organic shapes displayed on it. The two vases on the top shelf are by Jean Cocteau. Inspired by Picasso, after the war he

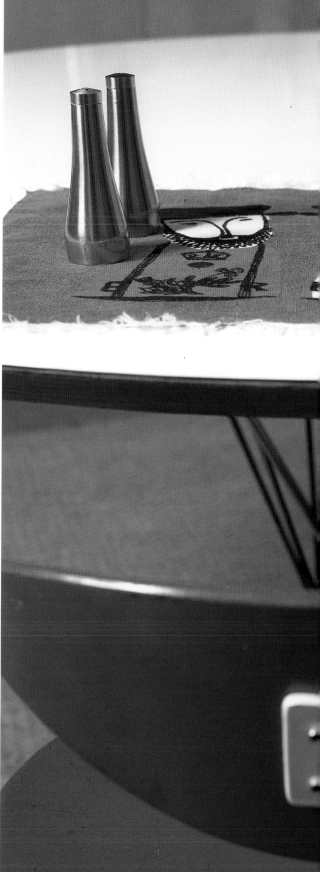

ABOVE A carafe and glasses from circa 1955 by Margaret Casson, who produced several designs for Chance & Co., inspired by science and astronomy.

RIGHT This dining table is by American sculptor-designer Isamu Noguchi, who produced a range of wire-and-formica tables for Knoll, circa 1955. It is set with a '50s linen tablemat by Robert Stewart and stainless-steel tableware designed by Robert Welch, whose sculptural Oriana cutlery was produced by Mappin and Webb in 1957.

FAR RIGHT A mug designed by Norman Makinson for Wedgwood to commemorate the Festival of Britain in 1951.

began to experiment with ceramics. 'Pottery provides me with more possibilities and satisfaction than painting, drawing or writing,' claimed the writer and artist in 1959. 'I'd give a good many well-known pictures for a beautiful pot.'

Much as ladies of the period, in their huge, bell-shaped skirts, wobbled perilously on their sharp stiletto heels, so, with chairs, the generous, organic curves of seat and back were supported on slender metal legs, their New Look silhouette reflecting wartime technology and the development of new materials. Laid out on Isamu Noguchi's table with its twisted wire base, Robert Welch's curving, abstracted metalware contrasts with Robert Stewart's linen, whose sketchy illustration is a typical example of period whimsy.

If chairs and tables almost seemed to float in space on their spindly supports, then space itself was an important influence on decorative pattern. Glassware and ceramics were adorned with astronomical imagery as well as futuristic buildings such as the Skylon and the Dome of Discovery – built for the 1951 Festival of Britain – which captured the optimistic mood of the moment and heralded the dawning of the space age.

Whereas the lines of the furniture are long, lean and architectural, the ceramics are curvaceous, capturing period taste for organic, asymmetric and sculptural forms, for which clay was a perfect medium.

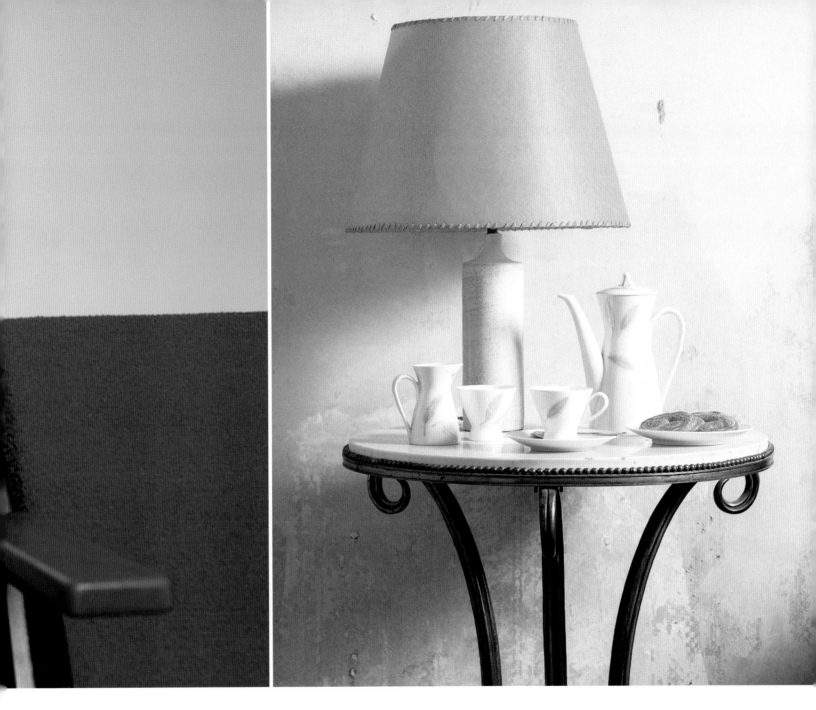

ABOVE FAR LEFT The large Peanut vase sitting on Robin Day's 1954 Interplan sideboard and the charger in the foreground were designed by Alfred Burgess Read for Poole Pottery. Employed by Poole in the '50s, Read introduced freeform, organic shapes and replaced traditional florals with delicate abstract patterns in subtle colours. The white bowls, created by Robin Platt and Cairn Young for Rosenthal, are inspired by '50s design.

ABOVE CENTRE '50s Rosenthal orchid vases designed by Fritz Heidenreich and a Macassar ebony lamp, designed by Alexandre Noll in 1959, stand on a sideboard by British architects John and Sylvia Reid.

ABOVE Under a 1955 lamp by Georges Jouve is Rosenthal's Service 2000, designed in 1954 by Raymond Loewy and Richard Latham. Echoing the New Look hourglass shape, it was one of Rosenthal's most popular lines.

This English home shows '50s styling at its most elegant. Set against chairs by designers Terence Conran and Robin Day, and a coffee table by sculptor Eduardo Paolozzi, this international array of tableware shows the latest in chic entertaining. The age of austerity has come to an end, and the scene is set for a postwar party.

The seating in this living room dates from the '50s and is by Robin Day, Britain's leading furniture designer of the period. The textile on the wall was designed circa 1954 by Marian Mahler for David Whitehead. The table, dating from around 1956, is inset with tiles by British sculptor Eduardo Paolozzi. It is set with modern glassware, a '50s Scandinavian enamelled metalware dish and, from the same period, a Midwinter bowl.

NEW ENTERTAINING

In many instances, rationing lasted far longer than war itself. In Britain, for example, it was 1954 before housewives could at last tear up their ration books and, after 11 years of food restrictions and the indignities of powdered egg and whale meat, they were ready for a bit of fun!

In the postwar period, eating habits became more informal and the choice of what to eat more exotic. Cookery writer Constance Spry opened her first book in 1956 with a chapter on cocktail parties – and everybody wanted to entertain. 'Buffet suppers and cheese and wine parties became all the rage,' remembers Marguerite Patten, one of Britain's first TV chefs, 'and the most important thing was that everything should look as decorative as possible.'

Manufacturers of tableware latched on to this desire for fun and frivolity. Midwinter, one of Britain's most pioneering ceramics firms, launched their Stylecraft line in 1953, followed by the Fashion line in 1954. 'You may "fashion style" your table with the latest tableware, just as you would buy the latest style in dress design,' claimed director Roy Midwinter. A number of Midwinter pieces are shown in this interior, including the 1956 pattern Plant Life, designed by Terence Conran and decorated with indoor pot plants, which – like elaborate flower arrangements – became a popular decorative craze in the '50s home. Period advertisements showed Plant Life plates covered with croissants, tapping into a growing interest in Continental foods.

'We have also fallen in love with food again,' wrote Terence Conran, noting that the process of marketing, cooking and choosing different equipment and tableware 'is again one of the great pleasures of life.'

THIS PAGE **The height of dinner-party chic: a Le Creuset fondue set and a Danish teak-handled dish serves up this 'exotic' cuisine. Stainless-steel tableware became popular during the '50s and '60s. The 1956 Plant Life plates are designed by Terence Conran for Midwinter, as is the Salad Ware sifter from 1955.** OPPOSITE **These Midwinter plates and bowl are from the Oakley range, designed by Jessie Tait. The metal-legged chair was designed in the '50s by Terence Conran.**

Similarly, on the other side of the Atlantic, the Kennedys had hired a French chef. And, within three months of its publication in 1961, the first book by American housewife Julia Child on French cooking had sold 20,000 copies. American women were discovering entertaining as an art form, and home cooking became increasingly adventurous. The flambés, soufflés and cream-laden gâteaux of the '50s gave way in the '60s to daubes, cassoulets and peasant-style cookery, rather than Cordon Bleu cuisine. The fondue was another favourite dinner party choice. Like the newly available foods and wines, tableware was imported from across the globe. Le Creuset's (established 1925) colourful French cast-iron casseroles became extremely fashionable in the '60s.

This interior includes German porcelain, Italian glassware and Danish metalware, reflecting both the international nature of contemporary styling and the huge wealth of objects available to the postwar homeowner. 'When did you last hear the word austerity?' demanded *Queen* magazine in 1959, announcing the arrival of 'an age of unparalleled lavish living…. It is the age of BOOM.'

LEFT Laid out on a 1954 Robert Heritage sideboard, ready for a buffet dinner, are plates and a cruet set from Rosenthal's 1976 Suomi range, designed for the German factory by Timo Sarpaneva. Alongside are two Hornsea vases and a '50s space-influenced lamp produced by the Dutch company Philips.

FAR LEFT AND BELOW A '50s butterfly chair and floor lamp (again by Philips) set the scene. The modern glassware on the left of the cabinet is by Italian designer Ettore Sottsass and the carafe is by Margaret Casson. On the table is a range of '50s bowls: a two-tone Melaware dish, a Krenit-ware bowl and a small Midwinter dish from the 1958 Patio range.

COCKTAIL HOUR

Popular in the '20s and '30s, and impossible during the war, cocktail parties returned to fashion in the '50s, when at last people were free to entertain again.

The postwar passion for cocktails stimulated a wealth of decorative domestic items. In the '50s, the home bar became an object of desire, with styles ranging from discreet rectilinear cocktail cabinets to elaborate novelty designs such as the boat bar, simulating the prow of the ship and coming complete with portholes and gilt-metal anchor.

Cocktail glasses were produced in multicoloured domino sets and decorated with everything from abstract patterns to bathing beauties. Pin-up girls (a term that emerged during World War II when soldiers pinned up girlie pictures in their quarters) were a favourite decorative motif on cocktail ephemera; other popular themes included gambling (playing cards and dice, for example) and animals, particularly poodles and cats.

In this interior however, kitsch extravagances are rejected in favour of a more sophisticated and intimate cocktail twist. The long '50s tubular Raye lampshade by French ceramicist Roger Capron hangs over a handsome Danish ice bucket, the thick-walled glass mirroring its frozen contents. Postwar glass designers took much of their inspiration from ice and snow. In 1969, Whitefriars

THIS PAGE **The ultimate accessories for a sophisticated retro cocktail party are here: tall, elegant amber glassware; a '60s Norwegian enamelled plate decorated with an Op-art pattern; the '70s Eiger decanter and drinking glasses from Whitefriars; '50s Krenit-ware enamelled bowls with yellow interiors; and a Midwinter Patio pattern plate designed by Jessie Tait circa 1958.**
OPPOSITE **A tall ceramic Raye pattern lampshade designed by french ceramicist Roger Capron.**

The perfect cocktail requires the classic cocktail glass – the stem should be long enough to protect the conical bowl from the heat of the hand, its opening wide enough to display a decoration or garnish.

launched their Glacier range of glass tableware, inspired by Scandinavian designers and reflecting the '60s fashion for textured glass. Similar in style, the Eiger drinking glasses and decanter were designed by Geoffrey Baxter for Whitefriars in the early '70s, the icy ridged surface created in a wax mould.

Vintage objects from the '50s, '60s and '70s combine seamlessly with contemporary pieces in this apartment, creating a cocktail of tableware. The shapes of the modern drinking glasses and, in particular, the chromium cocktail shaker, hark back to the Art Deco period. It was in '20s America – the jazz age – that the cocktail really came into its own, stimulated by prohibition and the fact that illegal, and often unpalatable, liquor tasted better when mixed with other ingredients. After repealing prohibition in the early '30s, Franklin Roosevelt mixed the first legal martini in the White House, and Nikita Khrushchev went so far as to call this powerful drink 'America's lethal weapon'. The martini captured the inspiration of designers as well as drinkers, its glass becoming a recognized symbol of sophistication in the '50s and '60s – to be hung in neon outside cocktail bars around the world.

OPPOSITE **A vintage soda siphon with silver mesh and modern cocktail glasses sit on a red enamelled tray made by Emalox in Norway.**
ABOVE **A Danish glass ice bucket with a wicker handle.**
ABOVE RIGHT **The Cylinda Line stainless-steel ice bucket, tray and corkscrew were designed in the mid-1960s by Arne Jacobsen for Stelton, Copenhagen. The cocktail shaker and jug are modern, but the period influences are clear.**

NORTHERN LANDSCAPES

Light and airy, this interior reflects
the Scandinavian Modern look that
became the height of international
fashion in the '50s and '60s.

'More beautiful things for everyday use' was the motto of the Scandinavian designers who rose to international prominence after the war. Climate was crucial to the development of the Scandinavian Modern style. Harsh weather conditions emphasized the importance of a warm, comfortable home, and ordinary domestic objects were required to be both practical and attractive. 'The Scandinavian has a word for it, "brukskunst" (useful art),' explained critic Eileene Harrison Beer. 'He believes that food for his body should be served on tableware handsome enough to be food for his soul.'

Culturally and geographically isolated, particularly during the war years, Scandinavian designers drew on their own heritage and surroundings. The Nordic landscape itself was a major inspiration. Organic shapes, native materials, and colours and textures reflecting earth, plants and ice are all classic features of Scandinavian design, combined with clean contemporary lines.

Pioneer of this humane Modernism was the Finnish architect Alvar Aalto. Commissioned to build the Paimio tuberculosis sanatorium in 1929, he rejected the metal furniture considered hygienic for such institutions, because 'psychophysically these materials are not good for the human being. Wood,' he declared, 'was better for the human touch'. Using cantilever techniques more usually applied to metal, Aalto developed a new range of mass-produced plywood furniture, such as the tea trolley (overleaf) which established processed wood as a perfect material for the modern age. The curvilinear biomorphic forms used by Aalto, both in furniture and other media such as glassware, became part of Scandinavian vocabulary in the postwar period.

While designers experimented with technology in their quest for economical mass-production, nature

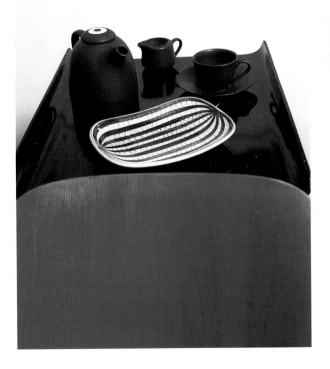

OPPOSITE **Large picture windows were a feature of '50s architecture, making the external landscape part of the internal decoration. This ideal is reflected in the organic shapes, colours and materials of the decorative ware on the window sill** (from left to right)**: a tall contemporary vase by Jonathan Adler; a small vase by Carl Harry Stålhane for Rörstrand; a wooden bowl by Dansk International Design; and a wooden bowl by Artiform, Italy.** ABOVE AND RIGHT **Glass from Holmegaard, Denmark, and striped ceramic bowls by Stig Lindberg for Gustavsberg, Sweden. The modern teapot is by Ö Design, Sweden.**

RIGHT AND BELOW **The white vases poised elegantly on George Nelson's '50s cabinet are by the modern American ceramicist Jonathan Adler. The ovoid vase resting on an Alvar Aalto table is by French designer Jean Besnard, and the stoneware bowl is by Carl Harry Stålhane for Rörstrand. Stålhane trained as an artist, and many of his designs in the '50s were inspired by abstract painting and sculpture. Charles Eames's 1946 moulded plywood folding screen complements the natural colours and organic forms.**

Scandinavian designers pioneered everyday tableware and furnishings that were handsome, affordable and practical. Combined, as they are here, with classic works by leading American and European 20th-century designers, these pieces, with their neutral colours and clean lines, create a look that is calm, elegant and humanely modern.

ABOVE The cane-handled porcelain teapot was designed by Ulla Procopé in 1957 for Arabia. The plate is by Stig Lindberg for Gustavsberg, decorated with the leaf patterns that the designer experimented with in the '40s and '50s.
LEFT The Model No 901 tea trolley by Alvar Aalto dates from 1935/36. The plates and salad servers are by Dansk International Design. Jens Quistgaard's teak VIII-8 ice bucket, also produced by Dansk, was designed in 1960 and is a masterpiece of streamlined modernism, and a perfect cocktail accessory for the contemporary living room.

'People work better, feel better and are happier when they have everyday objects of beautiful colours and shapes around them in their homes,' observed Swedish social reformer Ellen Key, 'regardless of how modest these objects may be.'

OPPOSITE The ceramics on the dining table are by Rörstrand (established in 1726). In the postwar period, the company became known both for handcrafted studio pottery and for colourful, contemporary tableware, such as the Redtop range, from which the casserole and bowl are shown here.

RIGHT The chair is by Charles Eames, reflecting his revolutionary experiments with moulded plywood in the '40s. The elongated wooden tray is by Dansk International Design.

and tradition remained important touchstones. In the '50s, Stig Lindberg created a range of colourful ceramics for Gustavsberg, many inspired by leaf patterns. Gustavsberg was typical of Scandinavian factories in that it produced commercial tableware and handmade studio pottery, combining the industry of the present with the artistry of the past. 'Handicrafts and industrial production go hand in hand,' advised Finnish designer Tapio Wirkkala. This policy was practised at Arabia in Finland and Rörstrand in Sweden, where brightly coloured oven-to-table ware (a '50s favourite) was manufactured alongside craft pieces. Holmegaard, under the designer Per Lütken, dominated the Danish glass scene after World War II, producing both series ware and experimental pieces in contemporary shapes and colours.

If there was one material more than any other that really summed up Scandinavian style, it was wood, particularly teak. Dansk International Design (established in 1954) exported Scandinavian-style wooden tableware and accessories across the world. Produced by Danish designer Jens Quistgaard in 1960, the VIII-8 ice bucket showed how solid teak could be sculpted into the most elegant modern shapes. It was this combination of contemporary lines with traditional materials that made Scandinavian design such an international success. 'It was very fashionable, but it wasn't scary,' remembers one homeowner who furnished her apartment in the early '60s with Danish furniture and Swedish tableware. 'It was comfortable, practical and a pleasure to live with.'

Half a century on, the '50s ideal of a dream American-style kitchen is still very much with us. This modern example mixes old, new and retro-inspired pieces to create a kitchen where appliances are not something to be hidden away, but objects to be celebrated in all their shiny, functional glory.

MODERN KITCHEN

After World War II, with the demobilization of their menfolk and the disappearance of servants for all but the most wealthy, women abandoned their wartime jobs and moved into the kitchen. 'This is the room which more than any other you love to keep shining and bright,' enthused a '50s *Woman's Own* magazine. 'A woman's place? Yes it is! For it is the heart and centre of the meaning of home. The place where, day after day, you make with your hands the gifts of love.' And not just with the hands, but preferably with the help of new 'labour-saving' appliances that became the ultimate objects of feminine desire in the '50s.

Contemporary advertisements showed women in party dresses, frilly hostess pinnies and high stilettoes grinning with delight as they pointed to their state-of-the-art cookers or washing-machines. '– and it's so much *fun* besides!' boasts a 1951 advert in *The American* for an automatic pop-up toaster. 'I love my New English Refrigerator,' trills one housewife in another typical period promotion. Perhaps more than any other room in the house, the kitchen was most affected by the postwar consumer boom.

The '50s also saw the introduction of the fitted kitchen and, thanks to the 'Magic of Plastic' (Formica surfaces, vinyl flooring), bright 'gay' colours replaced the pre-war hygienic whites and creams. The USA pioneered the powerful concept of the dream kitchen filled with modern machines 'to help you streamline

Though American in styling, this Dualit 4-slice toaster was conceived by British engineer Max Gort-Barten, who founded his company in the '40s. Its good looks blend perfectly with the shiny appliances of the modern kitchen.

your housework'. In creating mixers, blenders, juicers and other appliances, manufacturers used shiny chrome, bright enamels and bold, curvaceous shapes inspired by space rockets and automotive styling. As well as striving to make it more efficient, American industrial designers turned the kitchen into a glamorous place, and their effect can still be felt in the modern kitchen seen here, which mixes new and vintage to gleaming effect.

Contemporary objects such as the Master of Life juicer and Waring's Professional Blender clearly reflect the exuberance of American retro styling. Waring first began producing professional blenders for American soda fountains in the '30s, and with its geometrical lines, this blender shows an Art Deco influence that persisted in electrical goods in the '40s and '50s.

The electric toaster was invented by British firm Crompton and Co. in 1893, and the first pop-up toaster was produced in the USA in 1919. The Dualit toaster, seen here, created circa 1946 by British engineer Max Gort-Barten, was also inspired by American prototypes and, still in production today, is now regarded as a design classic. Features include a 'stay-warm mechanical ejector' and though originally designed for commercial use, it is now a popular domestic model.

Germany also paved the way in domestic product design. The '70s coffee grinder in this kitchen is by German manufacturer Krups (established in 1846), who, although famed for their rational approach, still could not resist the attraction of colour which today, as Luca Trazzi's modern blue coffee machine shows, we take for granted in the kitchen.

In creating fridges with 'fashion-coloured doors', and salmon-pink food mixers, '50s designers proved that white goods did not necessarily have to be white. They also showed that the kitchen could be not only a functional place, but also a fun and stylish one. 50 years on, equipped with modern and vintage items from around the world, the modern kitchen can still embody the same ideal.

Prohibition enhanced the attraction of the American soda fountain which, from the 1880s until the 1960s, was very much the social centre of small-town American life, particularly for teenagers. Thanks to film and TV, its appeal extended across the Atlantic. This selection of soda-fountain ice-cream glasses combined with a chromium bar stool reflects the enduring fascination of retro Americana. The Waring Professional Blender was also designed in the USA.

If '50s kitchens were all shiny chrome and colourful Formica, the '60s and '70s saw a return to a more natural look. With its wooden furnishings and handcrafted earthenware pots, this interior has all the components of a traditional farmhouse kitchen, combined with a truly modern awareness of style and space.

While '50s housewives revelled in the pleasures of plastic surfaces, processed food and labour-saving appliances, the '60s and '70s brought different aspirations. 'A possible reaction to a cold and clinical kitchen, new pleasures are to be found in baking bread, brewing beer and growing vegetables,' observed Terence Conran's *The Kitchen Book* (1977). 'People yearn to return to a self-sufficient life, but most want kitchens that combine efficient modern equipment with the old-fashioned virtues of a warm atmosphere and comfortable surroundings.'

Two of the figures responsible for inspiring this change were Julia Child and Elizabeth David. Elizabeth David was the most influential British cookery writer of the postwar period. From her first volume, *Mediterranean Cooking* (1950), David's books promoted not just traditional peasant dishes from France, but also traditional country cooking equipment: rustic clay pots, cast-iron casseroles, copper pans and wooden utensils – many originating from France.

Likewise, Julia Child's 1961 book *Mastering the Art of French Cooking* threatened the reign of TV dinners, meatloaf and corned-beef hash. In 1963 she took her talents to the small screen with *The French Chef*, extolling the virtues of copper pans to a yet wider audience of American women.

The crafts movement flourished in Britain after the war, particularly during the '60s, when shops such as the Craftsmen Potters Association in London became popular with a middle-class clientele in search of the good life, and an honest pot. This table is covered with stoneware crocks and storage jars produced by a range of different potters, all still active in Britain (from left to right): **a John Leach bread crock; bowls by Richard Batterham; Svend Bayer's lidded storage jar; a casserole by Andrew and Joanna Young; a bread crock by Richard Batterham; and a loop-handled jug by John Leach.**

HOMESPUN WARES

At a period when functional implements were hidden in Formica fitted cabinets, in the kitchen/dining rooms of Elizabeth David and Julia Child these everyday items were kept on open display, on pine dressers or hanging from the walls as in an ironmonger's shop. The look was subsequently adopted by fashionable '60s retailers (Williams-Sonoma in San Francisco and Habitat and Elizabeth David's own shop in London), and slowly filtered into the family kitchen. Chuck Williams, founder of Williams-Sonoma, wrote of the '60s, 'Julia Child's cooking show was finding an audience. She would show how to make a soufflé one night, and the next day people would come in asking about soufflé dishes.'

Through the use of natural materials, earth colours and traditional items, this kitchen harks back to an idealized rural past, while the uncluttered surfaces and sculptural forms show a keen awareness of modern design. Objects are arranged both so that they are practically to hand and in order to show off their individual forms. Colours are warm and harmonious, and the combination of wood, glass, pottery and metalware provides a variety of textures. 'The perfect kitchen,' wrote Elizabeth David, 'would be really more like a painter's studio furnished with cooking equipment.' And, some 25 years on, one feels she would have approved of the present interior.

THIS PAGE On the tabletop, the cast-iron candlestick is by British designer David Mellor, as is the coffee pot from the 1969 Au Pair range, in stainless steel with a coloured acetal resin knob and handle.
OPPOSITE On the coffee table is another coffee pot, again by Mellor, from the Pride range – made from silver with leather-covered handles.

'The craftsman who designs for mass production ... should create an object of sculptural worth with good proportions,' Jens Quistgaard

'Earthenware casseroles … should be in every household,' advised Elizabeth David, adding that cassoulets and daubes would lose 'flavour and a good deal of their charm if cooked in an ordinary saucepan'.

Set off by white blinds and walls, this corner is devoted to blue. The chair is by British designer Robin Day. On the table stands a decahedral kingfisher-blue Banjo vase made by Whitefriars Glass circa 1969 and designed by Geoffrey Baxter. Next to it is a blue glass Gulvase bottle by Holmegaard, dating from the '60s, a Scandinavian covered jar, and a clear blue Continental glass bowl and drinking glass.

Pale walls and stripped floors prove a fitting backdrop for a collection of brilliantly coloured, boldly shaped and richly textured decorative objects, reflecting the inventiveness of postwar design. By grouping objects according to colour, separate areas of interest are created in each room.

COLOUR PARTY

The cult of youth that directed music and fashion in the '60s also had its influence in the home, as the rainbow colours of contemporary clothing spread to the applied arts.

The decahedral blue glass Banjo vase on the living-room table in this apartment and the orange vases shown on the sideboard (*overleaf*) are by Whitefriars Glass. This new 'textured' range was designed by Geoffrey Baxter in 1966 and launched in 1967, the year of the Summer of Love, when colour became psychedelic. Vases were blown into textured moulds – the mould for the cylindrical Bark vases was actually lined with tree bark, forming an irregular, lumpy surface. The Banjo vase represents the more unusual, abstracted shapes that were also produced. All this glassware came in a variety of glowing colours – kingfisher blue and tangerine being added to the range in 1969, closely followed by meadow green and aubergine.

Next to the Banjo vase is a blue bottle vase by Holmegaard, one of Denmark's most inventive postwar glass factories. These bottles – or Gulvases – were designed by Otto Brauer from 1962.

THIS PAGE On the glass table is a selection of vintage continental glassware and ceramics, red in colour and extravagant in form. On the sideboard are white textured vases from Hornsea Pottery's Home Décor range, designed by John Clappison from 1959 to 1962. Clappison's works are becoming increasingly sought after by collectors today. The armchair and ottoman are by Hans Wegner, one of Denmark's leading furniture designers in the '50s.

OPPOSITE LEFT The mustard-coloured lamp stand is by Royal Doulton and stands alongside a selection of vintage American ice-cream cups.

OPPOSITE RIGHT A cylindrical Bark vase and two other tangerine vases from the Whitefriars textured range. Produced 1969–74, tangerine was an extremely popular colour.

They were produced in various sizes and came in a range of colours, and were made in both clear and cased glass. Their extruded, elongated shape was a feature of '60s design.

The collection of red vases is also typical of the period in the use of extravagant form, inspired by sources ranging from abstract sculpture to 19th-century pharmacy bottles to psychedelic posters. Designers prided themselves on their individuality. 'We make no traditional products,' John Clappison, design director of Hornsea Pottery proudly informed *House & Garden* magazine in December 1968. The ceramics shown here illustrate this variety in Hornsea's products: the white vases on the sideboard reflect period interest in textured decoration, while with the candy-striped Rainbow planters and the Springtime cruet set, the accent is firmly on colour and pattern.

'The Beatles really pricked the old fuddy-duddy balloon and the ripples touched and reshaped every aspect of our domestic lives,' ceramic designer David Queensberry told HOUSE & GARDEN magazine in 1968.

THIS PAGE The grey vases on the sideboard are by Hornsea pottery, the slipware pattern reflecting the factory's interest in producing textured ceramics. Also by Hornsea are the Summit mustard pot, with its stripy ribbed pattern, and the Springtime cruet set, in which three-dimensional decoration has been replaced by flat surface design. The dinner plates are by the Meakin factory, in the Studio shape which, designed in 1964, served as a base for a huge range of '60s patterns. The plate, far left, is by Midwinter in the bestselling 1966 Spanish Garden pattern, recalling the patterns of Islamic tiles and inspired by a Liberty print tie.

THIS PAGE **The planters and vase are from Hornsea Pottery's Rainbow range, introduced in 1961. Their pattern reflects the period desire for more colourful ceramics and a strong interest in textured decoration.**

Laid out in a modern kitchen, this Scandinavian tableware was produced in the '50s. Created for everyday use, half a century on these objects still fulfil their function perfectly, showing the enduring nature of good design.

SCANDINAVIAN UTILITY

If '50s America gave birth to the concept of the 'Dream Kitchen', filled with big, bold and colourful items, then a very different kitchen was dreamt up in postwar Scandinavia. 'I would like to design things that are so obvious that one hardly notices them,' claimed Finnish designer Kaj Franck, whose everyday tableware created what one '50s newspaper described as a 'revolution on the dining table'. Set on the table seen on this page is crockery from the Kilta range, Franck's most famous design, produced for Arabia in 1952. What made this service revolutionary was its simplicity and versatility. The clean, geometric shapes were stackable and multi-functional, and pieces could be used in the oven. Kilta came in a range of

OPPOSITE The crockery laid out on the table is from the Kilta range designed for Arabia by Kaj Franck in 1952, and the waisted green carafe was produced by Nuutajärvi in 1954, again designed by Kaj Franck. Both the glass pitchers and Kilta (now called Teema) remain in production today. The cutlery is by Arne Jacobsen and the one-piece plastic chairs were designed in the '60s by Verner Panton.

THIS PAGE The melamine Margrethe bowls in the foreground were designed in 1950 by Sigvard Bernadotte and Acton Bjørn. The bowls and pans behind are Danish Krenit ware, made from steel with bright enamel interiors; this colourful kitchenware has become highly collectable.

different colours, and customers were encouraged to mix and match rather than having to buy a full service at a time of national shortages. The undecorated earthenware was cheap to produce, affordable in price – and of course it looked good.

Franck applied the same principles to his utilitarian glassware. The waisted carafe he designed for Nuutajärvi Glassworks in 1954 came in several colours. The elegant shape, echoing the hourglass fashions of the day, resulted from his attempt to find a form that would avoid the expensive process of manufacturing a handle and that was slender enough to be held in one hand.

It is this stylish rationalism that lies at the very heart of Scandinavian design and that has made Nordic tableware so successful and so long lasting. Still in production today, the melamine Margrethe bowls by the kitchen sink *(page 93)*, were designed by Bernadotte and Bjørn in 1950. The team analyzed bowls from across the world in order to come up with this attractive, nesting design, which was strong, heat resistant and ergonomically shaped.

But Scandinavian design was not just about practical styling. This is, after all, the part of the world that gave us the plastic troll, favourite toy craze of the '60s. Designers met the '60s, in all its exuberance, head on. Marimekko – founded by Armi and Viljo Ratia in Helsinki in 1951 – became internationally famous for their boldly patterned, technicolour textiles, which, as well as being used for furnishing the home, were worn by every dedicated follower of fashion, right up to the American First Lady Jackie Kennedy. Combining the modestly rational with the flamboyantly decorative, this sleek interior encompasses this rich variety of Scandinavian style.

'Whatever it is, the Danes sell it, the Swedes manufacture it, the Norwegians ship it, and the Finns design it.'
Scandinavian saying

ABOVE **The Polygon coffee service above was created by Finnish designer Tapio Wirkkala for Rosenthal in 1973. Next to it stands a stainless-steel Au Pair coffee pot, produced in 1969 by David Mellor, who, like many British designers of his generation, was profoundly influenced by Scandinavian tableware.**
RIGHT **A collection of '60s Gulvase bottle vases from the Holmegaard glass factory in Denmark.**
OPPOSITE **The textile in the background was designed in the '60s for Marimekko by Maija Isola. The ceramics on the table are by the Swedish Gustavsberg factory and the steel and cane chair is by Danish designer Poul Kjaerholm.**

With its white walls, boldly geometric plastic furniture and shining stainless-steel tableware, this modern interior reflects the space-age look of the '60s. The conquest of the moon was the greatest technological event of the decade, and the visual vocabulary of space travel filtered down to earth, affecting everything from fashion to furnishing.

SPACE-AGE STYLE

THIS PAGE **Space-age colours and shapes are illustrated in a Danish teak-handled plastic ice bucket made in the '60s, and modern Finnish cups, by Arabia, set against Verner Panton's '60s stacking chair.**

OPPOSITE **Anna Castelli Ferrieri's Round-Up storage system, created for Kartell in 1969, supports a plastic thermos, creamer and sugar bowl designed by Erik Magnussen for Stelton.**

On 4 October 1957, the Soviet satellite Sputnik 1 orbited the earth in 96 minutes, stimulating a host of satellite-inspired items, from jam pots to cigarette boxes. The USSR had won the first stage of the space race, but it was the USA who put a man on the moon, and on 20 July 1969, an estimated 60 million people worldwide tuned in to watch the Apollo landing. Designers, too, caught space fever. A symbol of '60s optimism and undoubtedly the most glamorous expression of the Cold War, the space race had a huge effect on contemporary design, inspiring new technology and imagery.

In fashion, couturiers such as André Courrèges and Pierre Cardin sent models down the Paris catwalks in silver sequin trousers, white plastic boots and visored helmets. 'Courrèges invents the Moon Girl' enthused *Vogue* in 1964. As this interior demonstrates, domestic designers took up the baton, creating suitable furnishings for moon girls and boys in their vinyl and metal clothing. As in fashion, white and silver were favourite colours. Andy Warhol lined the Factory in New York with silver; and London's most swinging boutiques, such as Just Looking on the King's Road, covered their walls with polished aluminium. A cheaper alternative was to paper a room in your house with silver foil. 'It looked very "with-it", and it was fantastic for making your pot plants grow!' remembers one London journalist.

If metal was one fashionable material, another was plastic, perfect for space-age furniture. Italy designed some of the most inventive plastic seating of the decade, ranging from the blow-up chair to the vinyl-covered bean bag, both symbols of a new throwaway society. The Milanese firm Kartell (established in 1949) invested heavily in plastic technology. Designed by Anna Castelli Ferrieri in 1969, the Tondi or Round-Up

White and silver were the ultimate space-age colours, and plastic and metal the favourite shiny materials. Combined with strong geometric and abstract shapes, even everyday tableware took on a space-age look.

German company Nagel's '50s metal candleholders can be built into different patterns, mirroring atomic shapes and structures. Equally futuristic is Arne Jacobsen's stainless-steel Cylinda Line tableware, designed for Stelton in 1967. These strong geometric shapes sit perfectly against the abstract-inspired furnishings – Eero Aarnio's Pastilli rocking chairs and La Chaise (designed by Charles and Ray Eames).

As 'square' became a postwar term denoting old-fashioned, so rounded shapes emerged as a '60s favourite. Furnishings and tableware lost their straight edges in favour of globe forms which looked like astronaut's helmets.

storage system is one of the first series of furniture to be produced in injection-moulded ABS plastic. The system came in modular units that could be stacked together as storage cabinets or used separately as stools and tables, meeting a contemporary desire for flexible, more informal furnishing. Its cylindrical shape was a period favourite, reflected in the Thermos set designed by Erik Magnussen for the Danish company Stelton in 1977. Produced first in stainless steel (later in plastic), and including a lid that opens and closes automatically when the Thermos is tilted, this practical and stylish design proved Stelton's bestselling product.

Scandinavia further pioneered the development of plastic furniture and domestic objects. Verner Panton's stacking chair (designed in 1960 but not manufactured until 1967) was one of the first, successful, single-piece chairs. Coming in a range of bright, fashionable colours, its flowing form was only rendered possible through new advances in plastic technology. Finnish designer Eero Aarnio also used synthetics to create dramatic, modern forms. His 1967/68 fibreglass Pastilli chair was intended both for indoor and outdoor use and provided a space-age interpretation of the rocking chair. But it was in the field of domestic technology (lighting, radios, record players, televisions) that space-age forms really took off like a rocket. One of the most iconic designs of the period was the circular television, reflecting the shape of an astronaut's helmet. Inspired by the Apollo moon programme, British designer Arthur Bracegirdle produced the first globe TV set for Keracolour in 1969. The oval Aphelion TV set in this apartment was designed by Stephen Foster in the early '70s. Combined with this bold furniture is a selection of shiny stainless-steel tableware, including Arne Jacobsen's 1967 Cylinda Line coffee service and Sergio Asti's 1976 Boca cutlery. Whereas in the '50s stainless steel was brushed to give it a more muted appearance, in the '60s and '70s the look was polished and shimmering.

Popularized by cult TV series and films such as *Barbarella* and Stanley Kubrick's *2001*, space-age design is today extremely collectable – conjuring up the glamour of the '60s and providing a decorative symbol of that 'giant leap for mankind' when science fiction was turned into space fact.

LEFT This blue glass Provence bowl, dating from the '50s, was created by Danish designer Per Lütken for Holmegaard. RIGHT AND BELOW Resting on a modern plate, this stainless-steel Boca (Italian for 'mouth') cutlery was produced for Lauffer in 1976 by Italian architect Sergio Asti. The cruet set is from Arne Jacobsen's 1967 Cylinda Line service for Stelton. The Aphelion TV set was designed in the early '70s by Stephen Foster.

HIPPY HOME

With its swinging furniture and technicolour tableware, this interior is decorated in '60s psychedelic style. Flower power may have begun as an anti-materialistic movement, but its colourful imagery quickly spread from the hippy pads of Haight-Ashbury to high-street stores across the world.

'Gradually the with-it world of fashion has been extending its influence,' observed *Ideal Home* magazine in 1966. 'Not content with deciding the clothes we wear, fashions now have a strong say in the homes we live in as a result furnishing has become more fun – more lively and lighthearted.' A major youth fashion of the day was psychedelic style. Psychedelia emerged from the USA in the mid-'60s – most notably from San Francisco, capital of flower power and the hippy movement. Inspired by hallucinogenic drugs ('Turn on, tune in and drop out,' urged LSD guru Dr Timothy Leary), psychedelia affected everything from music to clothing and, as this apartment shows, filtered into the home. Textiles were perhaps the most successful psychedelic domestic products. You didn't have to take LSD to enjoy a vision of 'tangerine trees and marmalade skies' – all you needed to do was close the curtains!

For a young generation moving into bedsits, squats and student apartments, lightness and mobility were all important. Posters replaced pictures, and a salient

OPPOSITE **Hanging basket chairs were produced in many European countries and could be bought very cheaply. On the mirrored table is a '60s plastic ice bucket. The candleholder, designed by Graham Bishop, is decorated with a target motif, a favourite Pop-art symbol; and the placemat is covered with a swirling psychedelic pattern.** THIS PAGE **This glass bowl is attributed to Whitefriars, who produced a variety of coloured pieces in the '60s.**

LEFT These cups and canister are from the
Totem range designed in 1963 by Susan Williams-
Ellis for Portmeirion Pottery. Produced in various
colours (white is most sought after by collectors
today), Totem was the company's bestselling
design in the '60s.

FAR LEFT BELOW This Comfortable Corsets coffee
pot and sugar bowl are also by Susan Williams-
Ellis for Portmeirion. This is part of a group of
ceramics launched in 1965 decorated with 19th-
century prints and advertisements.

FAR LEFT ABOVE Tangerine was a popular '60s
shade, as seen in these period pieces: an orange
faience coffee set from Denmark; a floral cushion;
and a tin tray by Dodo Designs showing Britannia
seen through psychedelic eyes.

BELOW A set of bowls in the Madeira pattern
designed by Nicholas Jenkins for Midwinter in
1965. Decorated with Art Nouveau revival flowers,
the fabric is Prince of Quince, designed by Julia
Glynn-Smith for Conran Textiles.

feature of the hippy pad was the rejection of the traditional 3-piece
suite in favour of multicoloured floor cushions. Cane furniture was
another choice. Popular designs included the exotic Peacock chair
and the hanging basket chair seen in this apartment *(page 102)* – the
ultimate swinging seat, which was suspended from the ceiling or from
its own metal frame, was endlessly featured in magazines.

Colour and pattern were also crucial elements. The kaleidoscopic
tones and swirling designs featured on psychedelic posters and record
covers appeared on the most humble domestic items, from placemats
to biscuit tins. Orange, pink and purple were favourite shades, and
designers drew on a wide range of imagery. Portmeirion was one of
the most inventive British potteries of the day. Resting on the furry rug
are ceramics from the Totem range, its raised pattern inspired by both
primitive symbolism and Victorian tiles. Portmeirion also produced the
Comfortable Corsets range, decorated with prints from a Victorian
underwear catalogue. Nothing was sacred, and every image was ripe
for reinterpretation. Dodo Designs, a fashionable British company
specializing in Pop domestic products, produced a range of tinware
covered with traditional patriotic images in day-glo tones.

The late '60s saw a host of decorative revivals: Victorian, Art Nouveau and Art Deco; but as well as looking to the past, designers also drew influences from abroad, particularly Asia, favourite destination on the hippy trail. Illustrated among the group of tins on this page is a selection of black, pink and blue canisters in a Moorish-inspired pattern called Salome and produced by Ian Logan for JRM Designs in 1967. The diversity of these tins is typical of the period, and perhaps the keynote of psychedelic design is its cheerful and colourful ecleticism. One of the most successful designers of the period was Peter Max, who produced the Happy tray and also features on the front cover of *Life* magazine (5 September 1969). 'His art is a savoury rehash of Art Nouveau, Op and Pop,' noted the magazine. 'Max hopes his designs will bring happiness and harmony into millions of people's lives.' At the age of 29, the New York artist was already earning $2 million a year from his psychedelic patterns, which appeared on everything from clocks to napkins, epitomizing the mass commercialization of a once-alternative style.

'Alphonse Mucha, Max Ernst, René Magritte … Dulac, contemporary comic books, ancient book illuminations – all boiled down to make a visionary and hallucinatory bouillabaisse,' noted the OBSERVER in 1967. 'The whole world can be plundered for decoration,' agreed Richard Neville, founder of Oz magazine. 'Copyright is ignored.'

RETRO LOUNGING

In this postwar apartment, vintage tableware is used to reinforce a subtly retro look, bringing together elements from different decades and echoing shapes and colours of retro furnishing and decor.

This apartment is inspired by '60s and '70s style. Brown and beige were favourite colours in '70s interior decoration, ranging from the coffee-and-cream Art Deco revival look to the earthy tones and nubbly textures that reflected more rustic tastes. The continuing popularity of open-plan homes stimulated demand for modular seating, such as this sofa system that can be pushed into corners and adapted to the shape of the room.

'Because today's floor plans tend to be very open, traditional approaches to furniture arrangement no longer necessarily work,' advised *House & Garden's Complete Guide to Interior Decoration* in 1970. 'Sofas, chairs and accompanying tables often form islands of relaxation, subtly connected so that they can be enlarged, reduced or merged on occasion. Contemporary upholstered pieces are so low, they barely interrupt the sweep of space around them.' These low-slung furnishings – combined with developments in polyurethane foam – meant that designers could produce both enlarged and varied seating shapes for the home.

The pictures in this apartment recall '60s Pop art, and both their geometric patterns and the overall colour scheme of the space are picked up by the tableware. The '60s Focus coffee pot is manufactured by the British company Midwinter. Moving away from Midwinter's freeform shapes of the '50s, David Queensberry had introduced the straight-sided cylindrical Fine shape in 1962, inspired by the form of a milk churn and capturing the geometrical

LEFT **Barbara Brown's Focus pattern – originally conceived as a textile – was translated into ceramics, as seen on this coffee pot produced by Midwinter in 1964. The '60s design illustrated here in the bold, geometric pattern and form of the coffee pot is in stark contrast to the soothing organic curves of other ceramics in the apartment which belong to later decades.**
RIGHT **Modular seating systems were a popular feature of open-plan living arrangements. The candelabra on the table is by Platt and Young for Rosenthal.**

mood of the moment. Designer Barbara Brown had already produced a series of textiles for the London home-furnishing shop Heal's when, in 1964, she created Focus, her first work for Midwinter. Inspired by Op art, the grey, brown and black pattern of circles and squares proved a bestseller.

Op, Pop and Mod fashions affected tableware as well as clothing. In 1969, Burgess and Leigh launched their Orbit pattern. 'Fresh and scintillating as if from outer space!' boasted the advertisement. 'This thrilling new idea in modern tableware is a bold exercise in spatial relationships.' Orbit came in two trendy colour variations: green and blue, and orange and red.

Small wonder that after the extravagant and jubilantly psychedelic colour schemes of the '60s, in the '70s there was a move towards more muted, natural tones. For example, Timo Sarpaneva's Suomi service designed for Rosenthal in 1974, and shown on the dining table *(pages 112–13)*, relies not on colour for its effect but on sculptural shape, its compact organic forms inspired by the round, smooth pebbles on Finland's coast. While in the '60s designers embraced space-age technology and looked to the stars, in the '70s they came back down to earth again. The backlash against the exuberance and optimism of '50s and '60s Modernism began, and fashion moved towards the more traditional and conservative. Muted tones took over, with glassware in tobacco-smoke greys or glowing amber shades, and ceramics in soothing browns.

Hornsea pottery enjoyed considerable success in the late '60s and '70s with their brown ceramics, ranging from the country-kitchen-style Heirloom pattern *(page 82)*, to the more sophisticated lines of the Contrast tableware, introduced by Martin Hunt in

Circles within circles and spheres cut into cubes were typical of '60s pattern and form, and these shapes continued to fascinate designers into the '70s. OPPOSITE Orbit plates by Burgess and Leigh drew on Op-art imagery, while the modern dip tray beside them recalls sculptural designs that were popular in the '60s and '70s. LEFT The modern bowl beside the bed again recalls the period interest in geometrical shapes. In contrast is the black Denby Pottery freeform bowl below. BELOW This elegant amber glassware – made popular in the '70s – includes contemporary stemware by Bowles and Linares.

Circles, discs and target patterns became the height of decorative fashion in the '60s, appearing in Op- and Pop-art paintings, in contemporary clothes and jewellery and on everyday domestic objects.

ABOVE **This '70s smoked-glass carafe and drinking glasses set was made in Denmark. Smoked glass was a popular medium, both for tableware and in furnishings, with glass-topped tables a common feature in the '70s home.**

1975. In this apartment is a tea service in Hornsea's Lancaster pattern from the Contrast range, partially glazed in dark chocolate brown, black and white. The solid and chunky design is typical of the decade that gave birth to the platform shoe. The long slender cylinders of '60s tableware – as seen in Midwinter's Focus coffee pot – were replaced by shorter, squatter forms with thick curvaceous handles. Cutlery, too, changed shape in the '70s, as influential metalware designers such as David Mellor produced large, flamboyant shapes with broad shafts and boldly graphic blades, bowls and prongs.

Set in the brutalist architecture of a famous postwar apartment block (planned in 1959 and completed in 1972) this home is filled with vintage tableware that both enhances the decorative mood of each room and reflects the changing fashions of the '60s and '70s.

LEFT **This Suomi coffee service was designed by Timo Sarpaneva for Rosenthal in 1974 and manufactured from 1976. Its sculptural forms are made from porcelain and stainless steel. The vintage stainless-steel candlesticks are by Stelton, Copenhagen.**
ABOVE **This Lancaster tea service, from the Contrast range, was designed by Martin Hunt for Hornsea Pottery Company in England from circa 1975.**

ITALIAN INSPIRATIONS

Modern glamour is the key note of this Italian-inspired apartment, which combines strong architectural shapes with luxurious, sensuous materials. The elegantly monochrome colour scheme is interspersed with bursts of bright colour provided by Italian glass and metalware. The Italian design ethos of complementing art with industry was the formula for creating a look that was supremely beautiful yet perfectly functional. Here, hard and shining surfaces contrast with wood, leather and fur to create a variety of textures that are stimulating to the eye and comfortable for the body – the essence of LA DOLCE VITA.

Understated yet elegant modern furnishings – such as this modular seating designed by Antonio Citterio for B&B Italia in 1997 – provide a fitting backdrop to show off retro tableware. On the coffee table is the Bombé coffee set designed by Carlo Alessi in 1945. The stainless-steel ashtrays in the foreground were created by Achille Castiglioni for Alessi in 1970. The Perspex-and-chrome lamps were designed by Massimo Vignelli in 1965 and manufactured by Arteluce.

'In Italy,' claimed Gio Ponti, 'God made the plains, mountains, lakes, rivers and sky but the profiles of the cathedrals, facades, churches and towers were shaped by architects. In Venice, God created only the water and the sky. The remainder was made by architects.' Perhaps only an Italian designer could put God and architects on a level footing, but this statement certainly indicates the importance attributed to design and architecture during the reconstruction period in Italy. The country had been devastated by World War II and there was an immediate need for housing and domestic goods. Manufacturers exploited new materials and commissioned architects to produce everything from furniture to electrical appliances.

Architects and industrial designers received identical training in Italy, resulting in a close relationship between applied and industrial arts. The Espresso coffee machine, invented by Achille Gaggia in 1946, and the Vespa scooter, produced by Paggio in 1945, are perhaps the two most potent examples of this new aesthetic. Widely exported, these gleaming state-of-the-art objects symbolized not just Italian style, but the emergence of the teenage revolution, inextricably associated with coffee bars and scooters. Promoted by films such as Fellini's *La Dolce Vita* (1960), the Italian look became extremely fashionable, not

LEFT **These tall Oxford chairs were created by Danish architect Arne Jacobsen for St Catherine's College, Oxford. Completed in 1963, the college was Jacobsen's favourite project. The chairs, with their elongated backs, were originally designed for high table in the college dining room. These later versions have been upholstered in white leather.**

RIGHT **These colourful Murano glass vases were produced for Neo-Murin by master glassblower Malvino Pavanello.**

RIGHT **This tray was designed by Piero Fornasetti. After studying at the Brera Academy of Fine Arts in Milan, Fornasetti joined forces with Gio Ponti in the '40s. Ponti designed furniture; Fornasetti covered it with two-dimensional images to create a 3D effect. The surrealistic *trompe l'œil* style was to become his trademark for the next 40 years. Ceramics, magazine racks, textiles, even whole interiors were covered with black-and-white prints drawn from historical and contemporary sources. No object was too mundane to receive the distinctive Fornasetti treatment.**

just with Vespa-riding youths in their sharp Italian suits, but with style-conscious homeowners. *Domus* magazine, founded by Gio Ponti in 1928, provided an important vehicle for disseminating the work of new designers, whilst the Milan Triennale exhibitions helped to establish the city as the international capital of modern design.

By the early '60s, Italy had emerged as the world's leading exporter of modern furniture and furnishing, and this interior is filled with examples of Italian postwar design. Much of the metalware is by Alessi. Established in 1928, the company moved away from craft towards industrial design in the postwar period, experimenting with stainless steel and commissioning a range of celebrated architects and designers to work on their products. The ashtrays and cruet set created by Achille Castiglioni are typical Alessi artefacts: ingeniously practical (the ashtray has an internal spring to keep your cigarette from falling), blatantly shiny and self-consciously stylish. Lighting was another area in which the Italians excelled. The lamps in this apartment were created by Massimo Vignelli for Arteluce in 1965, an enlarged and boldly simple design in Perspex and chrome. Like many Italian architects, Vignelli worked across different media, designing everything from glassware to furniture to packaging.

While modern industrial design was an important aspect of La Linea Italiana, studio-based craftsmanship also flourished, particularly in Murano, traditional centre of Italian glass making. Designers combined age-old techniques with modern shapes and brilliant colours to create glass of astonishing energy and imagination.

'For an object to be only useful is not enough, each object should have a kind of poetry,' claimed the Italian graphic designer Piero Fornasetti, whose eclectic and fantastical prints, extremely popular in the '50s and '60s, decorated everything from tin trays to trash cans.

'Design is a global creative discipline with a strictly artistic and poetic matrix, and not simply one of the many tools at the service of marketing and technology to ensure improved production methods and better sales,' agreed Alberto Alessi. Perhaps what gave postwar Italian design its seductive appeal was this attempt to meet domestic practical needs not just with new technology and materials, but with an unembarrassed sense of artistry.

'I think that the success of so-called Italian design is due to the fact that design, in my opinion, is not a discipline but an attitude growing out of one's humanistic, technological, economic and political beliefs.'
Achille Castiglioni

ABOVE Italian designers embraced the new materials of stainless steel and plastic. The wire Citrus fruit basket designed by Ettore Alessi was produced from 1952, while the 9090 stainless-steel coffee pot designed by Richard Sapper was launched by Alessi in 1979. The modern cup and saucer were designed by Achille Castiglioni, also for Alessi. The '60s pyrex-and-plastic carafe and the plastic juicer by Thermozeta are also Italian.

LEFT This carafe and matching glasses are by French silver and tableware company Christofle and combine plated metal with Venini glass.

BELOW On this coffee table is an Italian clear and blue glass vase dating from the '50s and a Murano cased-glass ashtray.

OPPOSITE BELOW RIGHT These cruets for oil and vinegar with counter-weighted lids were designed by Achille Castiglioni for Alessi in 1980.

COLLECTING
RETRO TABLEWARE

Shopping for vintage objects is almost invariably more exciting than a trip to a modern department store. When you visit antique shops and flea markets you never know exactly what you are going to find. You might go out with the intention of buying a set of '50s Midwinter plates, and come home with a '60s Scandinavian glass vase because you saw it, you liked it, the price was right, and if you didn't buy it now, you might never see it again.

THIS PAGE **Finnish designer Timo Sarpaneva pioneered techniques in the creation of textured glass, as shown in the ice-like surface of this vase.** OPPOSITE **The glass carafe with a cane grip in place of the more conventional handle was designed by Kaj Franck circa 1955 for Nuutajärvi. The hourglass-shaped vase behind was created circa 1958 by Heinrich Löffelhardt for WMF.**

The collectables shopper has to be prepared to be flexible and, occasionally, courageous – but without being rash. The more you find out about your chosen field, the better you will buy, both in terms of quality and price. There is no substitute for handling objects. An increasing number of dealers and sale rooms are now focussing on modern design and looking costs nothing except time. Auction previews provide an ideal opportunity for hands-on learning – you are allowed to pick things up, turn them over and examine them in detail. Dealers are often happy to chat about their particular passion and, even if you're not buying, you can pick up a lot of information, visually and verbally, from simply wandering around antique fairs and galleries. And hopefully you will have fun, which is what collecting is all about.

Growing interest in modern design has stimulated a large number of books and catalogues, and pictorial guides are a useful source of reference. Many subjects have also acquired their own collectors' clubs, which provide an opportunity both to learn more and to meet fellow enthusiasts. The internet is a useful source for contacts and for comparing prices internationally. A growing number of sales now take place on the worldwide web, although before buying from a photograph and a description alone, it is important to know your subject – and to read the full terms of sale.

When buying a vintage item, examine it closely. Condition is crucial to value, and just as important if you are going to be using the object on your own table. Always ask for a receipt giving the name and address of the vendor and a full description of the item, including date and price. Prices will vary depending on current market trends – what's hot and what's not – and where you buy. The same object might well cost more from a specialist, metropolitan dealer than from a rural flea market, but what you are paying for is not just their rates and business costs, but the security and choice of stock that you would expect from an expert. But equally, much can still be discovered in car boot sales, charity shops and jumble sales. Objects often turn up piecemeal. Though you might not find a complete set of vintage plates or glasses, you can adopt period principles by mixing and matching different items, which makes for an interesting dinner table.

While fragile, rare or costly pieces might be kept principally for display, the majority of items featured in this book were designed for everyday use and are still being used today. Some additional precautions must be taken. Hand-painted china and wooden-handled cutlery were not created for the dishwasher and one of the sacrifices you have to make for style is a bit of old-fashioned washing up. But treat objects with due care and attention and they should last to decorate the tabletops of future generations of collectors.

One of the joys of collecting retro tableware is the sheer pleasure of hunting it down. There is plenty still available, and bargains can still be found. While many people continue to use the china, glass and metalware that they originally purchased in the '50s, '60s and '70s, others are chucking it out.

WHERE TO BUY

Key: t = telephone, f = fax,
m = mobile

COMPANIES WHO
SUPPLIED TABLEWARE FOR
PHOTOGRAPHY:

Alessi
22 Brook Street
London W1K RDF
t. 020 7518 9091
www.alessi.com

Boom
53 Chalk Farm Road
London, NW1 8AN
t. 020 7284 4622

Bowles and Linares
32 Hereford Road
London, W2 5AJ
t. 020 7229 9886
f. 020 7313 9689

Century
68 Marylebone High Street
London, W1 3AQ
t. 020 7487 5100
f. 020 7487 5168
shop@centurydesign.f9.co.uk

David Mellor Design
The Round Building &
Country Shop
Hathersage
Sheffield, S32 1BA
t. 01433 650220
davidmellor@UKOnline.co.uk

Fandango
50 Cross Street
London N1 2BA
t. 020 7226 1777
www.fandango.uk.com

Flin Flon
138 St John Street
London, EC1V 4UA
t. 020 7253 8849
f. 020 7253 8849

Freeforms
Unit 6, 58–60 Kensington
Church Street
London, W8 4DB
m. 07966 219 520
www.FreeformsUK.com

Gary Grant Choice Pieces
18 Arlington Way
London, EC1R 1UY
t. 020 7713 1122
choicepieces.co.uk

Origin 101
Gateway Arcade
Islington High Street
London, N1
m. 07747 758 852
origin101.co.uk

Places & Spaces
30 Old Town
London, SW4
t. 020 7498 0998

Rosenthal China (London) Ltd
c/o Josiah Wedgwood & Sons
Barlaston
Stoke-on-Trent
ST12 9ES
t. 01782 282915
f. 01782 271189
rosenthal.uk@wedgwood.com

Skandium
72 Wigmore Street
London, W1H 9DL
t. 020 7935 2077 shop

t. 020 7935 2088 office
f. 020 7224 2099
skandium@btinternet.com
www.skandium.com

Target Gallery
7 Windmill Street
London, W1P 1HF
t. 020 7636 6295
f. 020 7636 6295

The Home Service
Camden Stables Market
Chalk Farm Road
London NW1 8AH
m. 07779 793 065

Themes & Variations
231 Westbourne Grove
London, W11 2SE
t. 020 7727 5531
f. 020 7221 6378
go@themesandvariations.co.uk

Vessel
114 Kensington Park Road
London, W11 2PW
t. 020 7727 8001

OTHER RETAILERS
SPECIALIZING IN ORIGINAL
PIECES:

Alfie's Antiques Market
13-25 Church Street
London NW8 8DT
www.alfies.co.uk
t. 020 7723 6066

Atomic
Plumptre Square
Nottingham NG1 1JF
t. 0115 9415577

Eat My Handbag Bitch
6 Dray Walk
The Old Truman Brewery
91-95 Brick Lane
London E1 6RL
t. 020 7375 3100
www.eatmyhandbagbitch.co.uk
Postwar furnishings and
accessories focusing on
Italian, Scandinavian and
British design

Flying Duck Enterprises
320–322 Creek Road
London SE10 9SW
t. 020 8858 1964

The Ginnell Gallery
18-22 Lloyd Street
Manchester M2 5WA
t. 0161 833 9037

Igloo
34 Silver Arcade
Silver Street
Leicester LE1 5FB
t. 0116 251 4066

New Century
69 Kensington Church Street
London W8 4BG
t. 020 7937 2410

Planet Bazaar
151 Drummond Street
London NW1 2PB
t. 020 7387 8326

Sixty 6
66 Marylebone High Street
London W1M 3AH
t. 020 7224 6066

Squawk
51 Topsfield Parade
Tottenham Lane
London N8 8PT
t. 020 8245 3147

Stuff & Co
1 Heathcoat Street
Hockley
Nottingham NG1 3AF
t. 0115 988 1780

Tom Tom
42 New Compton Street
London WC2H 8DA
t. 020 7240 7909

Twentytwentyone
274 Upper Street
London N1 2UA
t. 020 7288 1996

Twentieth Century
Renaissance
Camden Stables Market
Chalk Farm Road
London NW1 8AH
t. 020 7603 1431

Visto
41 Pembrige Road
London W11 3HG
t. 020 7243 4392

OTHER RETAILERS AND
MANUFACTURERS OF
MODERN RE-ISSUES:

Abbot & Boyd
Chelsea Harbour Design
Centre
London SW10
t. 020 7351 9985

Aero
96 Westbourne Grove
London W2 5RT
t. 020 7221 1950

Aram Designs
3 Kean Street
London WC2B 4AT
t. 020 7240 3933

Ruth Aram Shop
65 Heath Street
Hampstead
London NW3 6UG
t. 020 7431 4008

b2
121 Water Street
Castlefield
Manchester M3 4JU
t. 0161 834 1113

Central
33-35 Little Clarendon Street
Oxford OX1 2HU
t. 01865 311141

Coexistence
288 Upper Street
London N1 2TZ
t. 020 7354 8817
www.coexistence.co.uk
Furnishings and accessories

The Conran Shop
81 Fulham Road
London SW3 6RD
t. 020 7589 7401
www.conran.co.uk
Call for branches

Divertimenti
45/47 Wigmore Street
London W1U 1PS
t. 020 7935 0689
www.divertimenti.co.uk

Focus on the Past
25 Waterloo Street
Bristol BS8 4BT
t. 0117 973 8080

Habitat
196 Tottenham Court Road
London W1P 9LD
t. 0645 334433
www.habitat.co.uk
Call for branches

Harrods
Knightsbridge
London SW1X 7XL
t. 020 7730 1234
www.harrods.com

Heal's
196 Tottenham Court Road
London W1P 9LD
t. 020 7636 2888
www.heals.co.uk

The Home
Salts Mill
Victoria Road, Saltaire
Bradford BD18 3LB
t. 01274 530770
www.saltsmill.org.uk
Furniture and homeware

Inhouse
28 Howe Street
Edinburgh EH3 6TG
t. 0131 225 2888
and
24-26 Wilson Street
Merchant City
Glasgow G1 1SS
t. 0141 522 5902

Jerry's Home Store
163-167 Fulham Road
London SW3 6SN
t. 020 7794 8622

Lloyd Davis Modern Living
14 John Dalton Street
Manchester M2 6JR
t. 0161 832 3700

Loft
24–28 Dock Street
Leeds LS10 1JF
t. 0113 305 1515
Showroom and design centre
featuring contemporary
furniture, homeware and
design

Nice House
The Italian Centre Courtyard
Glasgow G1 1HD
t. 0141 553 1377

Same
The Bridge
146 Brick Lane
London E1 6RU
t. 020 7247 9992

SCP Limited
135–139 Curtain Road
London EC2A 3BX
(also at Selfridges, London)
t. 020 7739 1869
www.scp.co.uk
Furniture, lighting,
kitchenware and accessories

Selfridges
400 Oxford Street
London W1A 1AB
t. 020 7629 1234
and
1 The Dome
The Trafford Centre
Manchester M17 8DA
t. 0161 629 1234
www.selfridges.co.uk

Shannon
66 Walcot Street
Bath BA1 5BD
t. 01225 424222
www.shannonuk.com
Scandinavian design products

Utility
85 Bold Street
Liverpool L1 4HF
t. 0151 7079919
www.utilityretail.co.uk
Contemporary homewares

Viaduct
1-10 Summers Street
London EC1R 5BD
t. 020 7278 8456
Top designers such as
Philippe Starck and other big
European names

Vitra
30 Clerkenwell Road
London EC1M 5PQ
t. 020 7608 6200
www.vitra.com
London headquarters of the
Swiss design company.
Manufacturers and retailers of
designs by Phillippe Starck,
Charles and Ray Eames,
Verner Panton and Antonio
Citterio

AUCTION HOUSES:

Bonhams & Brooks
Montpelier Street
London SW7 1HH
t. 020 7393 3900
www.bonhams.com
Call for regional and
international offices

Christie's
8 King Street
London SW1Y 6QT
t. 020 7839 9060
www.christies.com
Call for regional
representatives

Sotheby's
34–5 New Bond Street
London W1A 2AA
t. 020 7293 5000
www.sothebys.com

ARCHITECTS & DESIGNERS
WHOSE WORK IS FEATURED
IN THIS BOOK:

Echo Design Agency
5, Sebastian Street
London, EC1V 0HD
t. 020 7251 6990
f. 020 7251 6885
naomicleaver@echodesign.co.uk

VX Design
vxdesign.com

INDEX

Figures in italics indicate captions.

PICTURE CREDITS

All photographs by Thomas Stewart unless otherwise stated.

Key: **a** = above, **b** = below, **l** = left, **r** = right, **c** = centre

1 glass courtesy of Origin 101; **2** Stephen Shayler and Stephen Worth's house in Brighton; **4 above** glass courtesy of Gary Grant Choice Pieces; **4 below** glass courtesy of Origin 101; **10–11** plates courtesy of Themes & Variations; **12–13** Century 020 7487 5100; **14 al** Stephen Shayler and Stephen Worth's house in Brighton; **14 ar** tableware courtesy of Skandium; **14bl** Ron Wigham & Rachel Harding's apartment in London; **15** Target Gallery, London; **16–17** glass from Bowles & Linares and Vessel; **18–19 main** Target Gallery, London; **20–21** David & Fiona Mellor's house in Hathersage; **22** Target Gallery, London; **23 bl** David & Fiona Mellor's house in Hathersage; **23 ar 14bl** Ron Wigham & Rachel Harding's apartment in London; **24** Century 020 7487 5100; **25 a & b** Target Gallery, London; **26** plastic set courtesy of Skandium; **27al** tableware courtesy of Alessi; **27 r** *photographer Tham Nhu-Tran*; **28** Neil Bingham's house in Blackheath, London; **29 l** *photographer Tham Nhu-Tran*; **29 r** Century 020 7487 5100; **30 l & r** *photographer Tham Nhu-Tran*; **31** Neil Bingham's house in Blackheath, London; **32–33** Stephen Shayler and Stephen Worth's house in Brighton; **34 l** *photographer Tham Nhu-Tran*; **34 c** Stephen Shayler and Stephen Worth's house in Brighton; **35** Fake London Studio; **36 ar** bowl courtesy of Gary Grant Choice Pieces **36br** Century London 020 7487 5100; **37** Target Gallery, London; **38** Stephen Shayler and Stephen Worth's house in Brighton; **39 l** vase from Freeforms; **39 r** Neil Bingham's house in Blackheath, London; **41ar** bowls courtesy of Skandium **41br** *photographer Tham Nhu-Tran*; **42–43** Target Gallery, London; **44 inset & 45** *photographer Tham Nhu-Tran*; **44** Target Gallery, London, **46–48** *photographer Tham Nhu-Tran*; **49 a** Stephen Shayler and Stephen Worth's house in Brighton; **49 b** *photographer Tham Nhu-Tran*; **50–51** The T House in London designed by Ian Chee of VX Design, tableware left and right courtesy of Alessi; **52–55** Ron Wigham & Rachel Harding's apartment in London; **56 l** Ron Wigham & Rachel Harding's apartment in London, white dishes courtesy of Rosenthal China charger and peanut vase courtesy of Target Gallery, London; **56–57c** Ron Wigham & Rachel Harding's apartment in London, vases courtesy of Target Gallery, London; **57r** Coffee set courtesy of The Home Service, Camden Stables Market, London; **58–62** Neil Bingham's house in Blackheath, London; **62–63 main picture**, wall covering 'CANAS' by Arcadio Blasco for Gaston y Daniela, Madrid – UK distributor Abbot and Boydd, plates courtesy of Rosenthal China; **64 l** Yuen-Wei Chew's apartment in London designed by Paul Daly represented by Echo Design Agency; **64 cl & cr & 65** Rock, Victoria Embankment, London – 'think Studio 54', decanter and glasses courtesy of Gary Grant Choice Pieces, ice bucket courtesy of Flin Flon; **64 r** Neil Bingham's house in Blackheath, London; **66–67** Rock, Victoria Embankment, London – 'think Studio 54'; **67 l** ice bucket courtesy of Flin Flon; **68–73** Century London 020 7487 5100; **68** small vase courtesy of Target Gallery, wooden bowl courtesy of Origin 101; **69** ceramic dishes courtesy of Gary Grant Choice Pieces; **70 a & b** wide shallow ceramic bowl courtesy of Target Gallery **71 l & 73** ice bucket and wooden bowl courtesy of Origin 101; **71 r** dish courtesy of Gary Grant Choice Pieces; **74–79** David & Fiona Mellor's house in Hathersage; **86–91** Stephen Shayler and Stephen Worth's house in Brighton; **92–93** tableware courtesy of Skandium; **94 al** David & Fiona Mellor's house in Hathersage, coffee set courtesy of Rosenthal China; **94 b** bottles courtesy of Fandango; **96 l** lamp courtesy of Fandango, **96 l & 97** tableware courtesy of Skandium; **98** candelabra from Boom; **99** metalware courtesy of Skandium, **100–101** glass courtesy of Skandium; **101 b** Television from Places and Spaces **102–105** Fake London Studio; **102** metalware, **104 a** metal tray, **104 b** coffee pot, **105** material and **107** metal tray, all courtesy of Target Gallery, London; **106 al**

photographer Tham Nhu-Tran; **106–107 c** Target Gallery, London; **107** Fake London Studio; **108–113** Yuen-Wei Chew's apartment in London designed by Paul Daly represented by Echo Design Agency; **109** candelabra courtesy of Rosenthal China; **110** plates courtesy of Target Gallery; **111** glasses by Bowles and Linares, from Vessel; **112–113** white tableware courtesy of Rosenthal China **114–119** The T House in London designed by Ian Chee of VX Design; **114–115** lamps courtesy of Themes and Variations, ashtrays courtesy of Alessi; **116–117 c** vases, **117 r** metal tray courtesy of Themes & Variations; **118** and ashtrays **119** courtesy of Alessi; **119** vases courtesy of Themes and Variations; **119 inset** lamp and metalware courtesy of Themes and Variations; **120–121** Target Gallery, London.

PUBLISHER'S ACKNOWLEDGEMENTS

The publisher would like to thank everyone who helped to make the photography for this book possible. Particular thanks go to the Target Gallery, Neil Bingham, Ivan Barge, Gary Grant Choice Pieces, Ron Wigham and Rachel Harding, David and Fiona Mellor, Rosenthal China, Gaston y Daniela-Madrid and Skandium.